Cupid's Revenge by Francis Beaumont & John Fletcher

The English dramatists Francis Beaumont and John Fletcher, collaborated in their writing during the reign of James I of England (James VI of Scotland, 1567–1625; in England he reigned from 1603).

Beaumont & Fletcher began to collaborate as writers soon after they met. After notable failures of their solo works their first joint effort, Philaster, was a success and tragicomedy was the genre they explored and built upon. There would be many further successes to follow.

There is an account that at the time the two men shared everything. They lived together in a house on the Bankside in Southwark, "they also lived together in Bankside, sharing clothes and having one wench in the house between them." Or as another account puts it "sharing everything in the closest intimacy."

Whatever the truth of this they were now recognised as perhaps the best writing team of their generation, so much so, that their joint names was applied to all the works in which either, or both, had a pen including those with Philip Massinger, James Shirley and Nathan Field.

The first Beaumont and Fletcher folio of 1647 contained 35 plays; 53 plays were included in the second folio in 1679. Other works bring the total plays in the canon to about 55. However there appears here to have been some duplicity on the account of the publishers who seemed to attribute so many to the team. It is now thought that the work between solely by Beaumont and Fletcher amounts to approximately 15 plays, though of course further works by them were re-worked by others and the originals lost.

After Beaumont's early death in 1616 Fletcher continued to write and, at his height was, by many standards, the equal of Shakespeare in popularity until his own death in 1625.

Index of Contents

MEN

Cupid.
Leontius, the old Duke of Lycia.
Leucippus, Son to the Duke.
Ismenus, Nephew to the Duke.
Telamon, a Lycian Lord.
Dorialus   }
Agenor   } Courtiers.
Nisus   }
Timantus, a villainous Sycophant.
The Priest of Cupid.
Four young Men and Maids.
Nilo, sent in Commission to pull down Cupid's Image.
Zoylus, Leucippus's Dwarf.
Four Citizens.

WOMEN

Hidaspes, Daughter to the Duke.
Cleophila, and Hero her Attendants.
Bacha, a Strumpet.
Urania, her Daughter.
Bacha's Maid.
Urania's Maid.
Servants and Attendants.

ACTUS PRIMUS

SCÆNA PRIMA

Enter **DORIALUS**, **AGENOR**, **NISUS**.

AGENOR

Trust me my Lord Dorialus, I had mist of this, if you had not call'd me; I thought the Princesses birth-day had been to morrow.

NISUS

Why, did your Lordship sleep out the day?

DORIALUS

I marvel what the Duke meant to make such an idle vow.

NISUS

Idle, why?

DORIALUS

Is't not idle, to swear to grant his Daughter any thing she shall ask on her birth-day? she may ask an impossible thing: and I pray heaven she do not ask an unfit thing at one time or other; 'tis dangerous trusting a mans vow upon the discretion on's Daughter.

AGENOR
I wonder most at the Marquis her Brother, who is always vehemently forward to have her desires granted.

DORIALUS
He's acquainted with 'em before.

AGENOR
She's doubtless very chaste and virtuou.

DORIALUS
So is Leucippus her brother.

NISUS
She's twenty year old, I wonder
She aske not a Husband.

DORIALUS
That were a folly in her; having refus'd all the
Great Princes in one part of the world;
She'll die a Maid.

AGENOR   ʻ
She may ask but one, may she?

NISUS
A hundred times this day if she will;
And indeed, every day is such a day, for though
The Duke has vow'd it only on this day,
He keeps it every day: he can deny
Her nothing.

[Cornets.

[Enter **HIDASPES, LEUCIPPUS, LEONTIUS, TIMANTAS, TELLAMON.**

LEONTIUS
Come fair Hidaspes, thou art
Duchess to day,
Art thou prepar'd to aske, thou knowest
My oath will force performance.
And Leucippus, if she now ask ought that shall,
Or would have performance
After my death, when by the help of heaven,

This Land is thine, accursed be thy race,
May every one forget thou art my Son,
And so their own obedience.

LEUCIPPUS
Mighty Sir,
I do not wish to know that fatal hour,
That is to make me King, but if I do,
I shall most hastily, (and like a Son)
Perform your grants to all, chiefly to her:
Remember that you aske what we
Agreed upon.

LEONTIUS
Are you prepar'd? then speak.

HIDASPES
Most Royal Sir, I am prepar'd,
Nor shall my Will exceed a Virgins bounds,
What I request shall both at once bring
Me a full content.

LEONTIUS
So it ever does:
Thou only comfort of my feeble age,
Make known thy good desire,
For I dare swear thou lov'st me.

HIDASPES
This is it I beg,
And on my knees. The people of your Land,
The Lycians, are through all the Nations
That know their name, noted to have in use
A vain and fruitless superstition;
So much more hateful, that it bears the shew
Of true Religion, and is nothing else
But a false-pleasing bold lasciviousness.

LEONTIUS
What is it?

HIDASPES
Many ages before this,
When every man got to himself a Trade,
And was laborious in that chosen course,
Hating an idle life, far worse than death:
Some one that gave himself to Wine and Sloth,
Which breed lascivious thoughts;

And found himself conjoyn'd
For that by every painful man,
To take his stain away, fram'd to himself
A god, whom he pretended to obey,
In being thus dishonest, for a name
He call'd him Cupid
This created god,
Mans nature being ever credulous
Of any vice that takes part with his blood,
Had ready followers enow: and since
In every age they grew, especially
Amongst your Subjects, who do yet remain
Adorers of that drowsie Deitie:
Which drink invented: and the winged Boy,
(For so they call him) has his sacrifices.
These loose naked statues through the Land,
And in every Village, nay the palace
Is not free from 'em. This is my request,
That these erected obscene Images
May be pluckt down and burnt: and every man
That offers to 'em any sacrifice, may lose his life.

LEONTIUS
But be advis'd my fairest daughter, if he be
A god, he will express it upon thee my child:
Which heaven avert.

LEUCIPPUS
There is no such power:
But the opinion of him fills the Land
With lustful sins: every young man and maid
That feel the least desire to one another,
Dare not suppress it, for they think it is
Blind Cupid's motion: and he is a god.

LEONTIUS
This makes our youth unchaste. I am resolv'd:
Nephew Ismenus, break the Statues down
Here in the Palace, and command the City
Do the like, let proclamations
Be drawn, and hastily sent through the Land
To the same purpose.

ISMENUS
Sir, I will break down none my self,
But I will deliver your command:
Hand I will have none in't, for I like it not.

LEONTIUS

Goe and command it. Pleasure of my life,
Wouldst thou ought else? make many thousand suits,
They must and shall be granted.

HIDASPES

Nothing else.

[Exit **ISMENUS**.

LEONTIUS

But go and meditate on other suits,
Some six days hence I'll give thee Audience again,
And by a new oath, bind my self to keep it:
Ask largely for thy self, dearer than life
In whom I may be bold to call my self,
More fortunate than any in my age,
I will deny thee nothing.

LEUCIPPUS

'Twas well done, Sister.

[Exeunt all but these three **LORDS**.

NISUS

How like you this request my Lords?

DORIALUS

I know not yet, I am so full of wonder,
We shall be gods our selves shortly,
And we pull 'em out of Heaven o' this fashion.

AGENOR

We shall have wenches now when we can
Catch 'em, and we transgress thus.

NISUS

And we abuse the gods once, 'tis a Justice
We should be held at hard meat: for my part,
I'll e'en make ready for mine own affection,
I know the god incenst must send a hardness
Through all good Womens hearts, and then we have
Brought our Eggs and Muskadine to a fair Market:
Would I had giv'n a 100 l. for a tolleration,
That I might but use my conscience in mine
Own house.

DORIALUS

The Duke he's old and past it, he would
Never have brought such a plague upon the Land else,
'Tis worse than Sword and Famine:
Yet to say truth, we have deserv'd it, we have liv'd
So wickedly, every man at his Livery, and wou'd that
Wou'd have suffic'd us: we murmur'd at this
Blessing, that was nothing; and cry'd out to the
God for endless pleasures, he heard us,
And supplied us, and our Women were new still
As we need 'em: yet we like beasts still cry'd,
Poor men can number their woers, give us
Abundance: we had it, and this curse withal.

AGENOR
Berlady we are like to have a long Lent on't,
Flesh shall be flesh: now Gentlemen I had rather
Have anger'd all the gods, than that blind Gunner.
I remember once the people did but slight him
In a sacrifice: and what followed?
Women kept their houses, grew good huswives
Honest forsooth! was not that fine?
Wore their own faces,
Though they wear gay cloaths without surveying,
And which was most lamentable,
They lov'd their Husbands.

NISUS
I do remember it to my grief,
Young Maids were as cold as Cowcumbers
And much of that complexion:
Bawds were abolisht: and, to which misery
It must come again,
There were no Cuckolds,
Well, we had need pray to keep these
Divels from us,
The times grow mischievous.
There he goes, Lord!

[Enter one with an Image.

This is a sacriledge I have not heard of:
Would I were gelt, that I might not
Feel what follows.

AGENOR
And I too. You shall see within these
Few years, a fine confusion i'the Countrey: mark it:
Nay, and we grow for to depose the Powers,

And set up Chastity again, well, I have done.
A fine new goddess certainly, whose blessings
Are hunger and hard beds.

NISUS
This comes of fulness, a sin too frequent with us
I believe now we shall find shorter commons.

DORIALUS
Would I were married, somewhat has some favour;
The race of Gentry will quite run out now,
'Tis only left to Husbands, if younger Sisters
Take not the greater charity, 'tis lawful.

AGENOR
Well, let come what will come,
I am but one, and as the plague falls,
I'll shape my self: If Women will be honest, I'll be sound.
If the god be not too unmerciful,
I'll take a little still, where I can get it,
And thank him, and say nothing.

NISUS
This ill wind yet may blow the City good,
And let them, (if they can) get their own children,
They have hung long enough in doubt, but howsoever, the
old way was the surer, then they had 'em.

DORIALUS
Farewel my Lords, I'll e'en take up what Rent I can
before the day, I fear the year will fall out ill.

AGENOR
We'll with you Sir: And love so favour us,
As we are still thy servants. Come my Lords;
Let's to the Duke, and tell him to what folly
His doting now has brought him.

[Exeunt.

[Enter **PRIEST** of Cupid, with four young **MEN** and **MAIDS**.

PRIEST
Come my children, let your feet,
In an even measure meet:
And your chearful voices rise,
For to present this Sacrifice;
Lo great Cupid, in whose name,

I his Priest begin the same.
Young men take your Loves and kiss,
Thus our Cupid honour'd is
Kiss again, and in your kissing,
Let no promises be missing:
Nor let any Maiden here,
Dare to turn away her ear,
Unto the whisper of her Love,
But give Bracelet, Ring or Glove,
As a token to her sweeting,
Of an after secret meeting:
Now boy sing to stick our hearts
Fuller of great Cupid's darts.

SONG.

Lovers rejoyce, your pains shall be rewarded,
The god of Love himself grieves at your crying:
No more shall frozen honor be regarded,
Nor the coy faces of a Maids denying.
No more shall Virgins sigh, and say we dare not,
For men are false, and what they do they care not,
All shall be well again, then do not grieve,
Men shall be true, and Women shall believe.

Lovers rejoyce, what you shall say henceforth.
When you have caught your Sweet-hearts in your arms,
It shall be accounted Oracle, and Worth:
No more faint-hearted Girls shall dream of harms,
And cry they are too young, the god hath said,
Fifteen shall make a Mother of a Maid:
Then wise men, pull your Roses yet unblown,
Love hates the too ripe fruit that falls alone.

The Measure.

[After the Measure, Enter **NILO** and **OTHERS**.

NILO
No more of this: here break your Rights for ever,
The Duke commands it so; Priest do not stare,
I must deface your Temple, though unwilling,
And your god Cupid here must make a Scare-crow
For any thing I know, or at the best,
Adorn a Chimney-piece.

PRIEST
Oh Sacriledge unheard of!

NILO

This will not help it, take down the Images
And away with 'em.
Priest, change your coat you had best, all service now
Is given to men: Prayers above their hearing
Will prove but bablings: learn to lye and thrive,
'Twill prove your best profession: for the gods,
He that lives by 'em now, must be a beggar.
There's better holiness on earth they say,
Pray God it ask not greater sacrifice. Go home,
And if your god be not deaf as well as blind,
He will make some smoak for it.

GENTLEMAN

Sir—

NILO

Gentlemen, there is no talking,
This must be done and speedily;
I have commission that I must not break.

GENTLEMAN

We are gone, to wonder what shall follow.

NILO

On to the next Temple.

[Exeunt.

[Cornets. Descendit **CUPID**.

CUPID

Am I then scorn'd? is my all-doing Will
And Power, that knows no limit, nor admits none,
Now look'd into by less than gods? and weak'ned
Am I, whose Bow struck terror through the earth,
No less than Thunder, and in this, exceeding
Even gods themselves; whose knees before my Altars
Now shook off; and contemn'd by such, whose lives
Are but my recreation! anger rise
My sufferance and my self are made the subject
Of sins against us. Go thou out displeasure,
Displeasure of a great god, flying thy self
Through all this Kingdom: sow what ever evils
Proud flesh is taking of, amongst these Rebels:
And on the first heart that despise my Greatness,
Lay a strange misery, that all may know

Cupid's revenge is mighty; with his Arrow
Hotter than plagues or mine own anger, will I
Now nobly right my self: nor shall the prayers
Nor sweete smoaks on my Altars hold my hand,
Till I have left this a most wretched Land.

[Exit.

[Enter **HIDASPES** and **CLEOPHILA**.

HIDASPES
Cleophila, what was he that went hence?

CLEOPHILA
What means your Grace now?

HIDASPES
I mean that handsome man,
That something more than man I met at door.

CLEOPHILA
Here was no handsome man,

HIDASPES
Come, he's some one
You would preserve in private, but you want
Cunning to do it, and my eyes are sharper
Than yours, and can with one neglecting glance,
See all the graces of a man. Who was't?

CLEOPHILA
That went hence now?

HIDASPES
That went hence now, I, he.

CLEOPHILA
Faith here was no such one as your Grace thinks.
Zoylous your Brothers Dwarf went out but now.

HIDASPES
I think 'twas he: how bravely he past by:
Is he not grown a goodly Gentleman?

CLEOPHILA
A goodly Gentleman, Madam?
He is the most deformed fellow i'the Land.

HIDASPES

Oh blasphemy: he may perhaps to thee
Appear deform'd, for he is indeed
Unlike a man: his shape and colours are
Beyond the Art of Painting; he is like
Nothing that we have seen, yet doth resemble
Apollo, as I oft have fancied him,
When rising from his bed, he stirs himself
And shakes day from his hair.

CLEOPHILA

He resembles Apollo's Recorder.

HIDASPES

Cleophila, go send a Page for him,
And thou shalt see thy error, and repent.

[Exit **CLEOPHILA**.

Alas, what do I feel, my bloud rebells,
And I am one of those I us'd to scorn,
My Maiden-thoughts are fled against my self,
I harbor Traitors in my Virginity,
That from my Childhood kept me company,
Is heavier than I can endure to bear:
Forgive me Cupid, for thou art a god,
And I a wretched creature; I have sinn'd,
But be thou merciful, and grant that yet
I may enjoy what thou wilt have me, Love.

[Enter **CLEOPHILA** and **ZOYLUS**.

CLEOPHILA

Zoylous is here Madam.

HIDASPES

He's there indeed.
Now be thine own Judge; see thou worse than mad,
Is he deformed? look upon those eyes,
That let all pleasure out into the world,
Unhappy that they cannot see themselves;
Look on his hair, that like so many beams,
Streaking the East, shoot light o'er half the world,
Look on him altogether, who is made
As if two Natures had contention
About their skill, and one had brought forth him.

ZOYLUS

Ha, ha, ha: Madam, though Nature
Hath not given me so much
As others in my outward shew;
I bear a heart as loyal unto you
In this unsightly body (which you please
To make your mirth) as many others do
That are far more befriended in their births;
Yet I could wish my self much more deformed
Than yet I am, so I might make your Grace
More merry than you are, ha, ha, ha.

HIDASPES
Beshrew me then if I be merry;
But I am content whilst thou art with me:
Thou that art my Saint:
By hope of whose mild favour I do live
To tell thee so: I pray thee scorn me not;
Alas what can it add unto thy worth
To triumph over me, that am a Maid,
Without deceit? whose heart doth guide her tongue,
Drown'd in my passions; yet I will take leave
To call it reason that I dote on thee.

CLEOPHILA
The Princess is besides her Grace I think,
To talk thus with a fellow that will hardly
Serve i'th' dark when one is drunk.

HIDASPES
What answer wilt thou give me?

ZOYLUS
If it please your Grace to jest on, I can abide it.

HIDASPES
If it be jest, not to esteem my life,
Compar'd with thee: If it be jest in me,
To hang a thousand kisses in an hour
Upon those Lips, and take 'em off again:
If it be jest for me to marry thee,
And take obedience on me whilst I live:
Then all I say is jest:
For every part of this, I swear by those
That see my thoughts, I am resolv'd to do,
And I beseech thee, by thine own white hand,
(Which pardon me, that I am bold to kiss
With so unworthy Lips) that thou wilt swear
To marry me, as I do here to thee,

Before the face of heaven.

ZOYLUS
Marry you? ha, ha, ha.

HIDASPES
Kill me or grant, wilt thou not speak at all?

ZOYLUS
Why I will do your Will for ever.

HIDASPES
I ask no more: but let me kiss that mouth
That is so merciful; that is my will:
Next go with me before the King in haste,
That is my Will; where I will make our Peers
Know, that thou art their better.

ZOYLUS
Ha, ha, ha, that is fine, ha, ha, ha.

CLEOPHILA
Madam, what means your Grace?
Consider for the love of Heaven to what
You run madly; will you take this Viper
Into your bed?

HIDASPES
Away, hold off thy hands:
Strike her sweet Zoylous, for it is my Will,
Which thou hast sworn to doe.

ZOYLUS
Away for shame.
Know you no manners: ha, ha, ha.

[Exit.

CLEOPHILA
Thou know'st none I fear,
This is just Cupid's Anger, Venus look down mildly on us:
And command thy Son to spare this Lady once, and let me
Be in love with all: and none in love with me.

[Exit.

[Enter **ISMENUS** and **TIMANTUS**.

TIMANTUS
Is your Lordship for the Wars this Summer?

ISMENUS
Timantus, wilt thou go with me?

TIMANTUS
If I had a Company, my Lord.

ISMENUS
Of Fidlers: Thou a company?
No, no, keep thy Company at home, and cause cuckolds:
The Wars will hurt thy face, there's no Semsters,
Shoomakers, nor Taylors, nor Almond-milk i'th' morning,
Nor poach'd Egs to keep your worship soluble,
No man to warm your Shirt, and blow your Roses:
Nor none to reverence your round lace Breeches:
If thou wilt needs goe, and goe thus,
Get a Case for thy Captainship, a shower will spoil thee else.
Thus much for thee.

TIMANTUS
Your Lordship's wondrous witty, very pleasant believe't.

[Exit.

[Enter **TELAMON, DORIALUS, AGENOR, NISUS, LEONTI.**

LEONTIUS
No news yet of my Son?

TELAMON
Sir, there be divers out in search:
No doubt they'll bring the truth where he is,
Or the occasion that led him hence.

TIMANTUS
They have good eyes then.

LEONTIUS
The gods goe with them:
Who be those that wait there?

TELAMON
The Lord Ismenus, your General, for his dispatch.

LEONTIUS
Oh Nephew: we have no use to imploy your

Virtue in our War: now the Province is well setled.
Hear you aught of the Marquis?

ISMENUS
No Sir.

LEONTIUS
'Tis strange he should be gone thus:
These five days he was not seen.

TIMANTUS
I'll hold my life, I could bolt him in an hour:

LEONTIUS
Where's my Daughter?

DORIALUS
About the purging of the Temples, Sir.

LEONTIUS
She's chaste and virtuous; fetch her to me,
And tell her I am pleas'd to grant her now
Her last request, without repenting me.

[Exit **NISUS**.

Be it what it will: she is wise, Dorialus
And will not press me farther than a Father.

DORIALUS
I pray the best may follow; yet if your Grace
Had taken the opinions of your people,
At least of such, whose wisdoms ever wake
About your safety, I may say it, Sir,
Under your noble pardon: that this change
Either had been more honor to the gods,
Or I think not at all. Sir, the Princess.

[Enter **HIDASPES**, **NISUS** and **ZOYLUS**.

LEONTIUS
Oh my Daughter, my health!
And did I say my soul, I ly'd not;
Thou art so near me, speak, and have whatever
Thy wise Will leads thee too: had I a Heaven,
It were too poor a place for such a goodness.

DORIALUS

What's here?

AGENOR
An Apes skin stuft I think, 'tis so plump.

HIDASPES
Sir, you have past your word,
Still be a Prince, and hold you to it.
Wonder not I press you, my life lies in your word:
If you break that, you have broke my heart, I must ask
That's my shame, and your Will must not deny me:
Now for Heaven be not forsworn.

LEONTIUS
By the gods I will not,
I cannot, were there no other power,
Than my love call'd to a witness of it.

DORIALUS
They have much reason to trust,
You have forsworn one of 'em out o'th' countrey already.

HIDASPES
Then this is my request: This Gent.
Be not ashamed, Sir:
You are worth a Kingdom.

LEONTIUS
In what?

HIDASPES
In the way of marriage.

LEONTIUS
How?

HIDASPES
In the way of marriage, it must be so,
Your oath is ti'd to Heaven: as my love to him.

LEONTIUS
I know thou dost but try my age,
Come ask again.

HIDASPES
If I should ask all my life-time, this is all still.
Sir, I am serious, I must have this worthy man without
enquiring why; and suddenly, and freely:

Doe not look for reason or obedience in my words:
My love admits no wisdom:
Only haste, and hope hangs on my fury,
Speak Sir, speak, but not as a Father,
I am deaf and dull to counsel: inflamed blood
Hears nothing but my Will;
For Gods sake speak.

DORIALUS
Here's a brave alteration.

NISUS
This comes of Chastity.

HIDASPES
Will not you speak Sir?

AGENOR
The god begins his vengeance; what a sweet youth
he has sent us here, with a pudding in's belly!

LEONTIUS
Oh let me never speak,
Or with my words let me speak out my life;
Thou power abus'd: great Love, whose vengeance now we
feel and fear, have mercy on this Land.

NISUS
How does your Grace?

LEONTIUS
Sick, very sick I hope.

DORIALUS
Gods comfort you.

HIDASPES
Will not you speak? is this your Royal word?
Do not pull perjurie upon your soul.
Sir, you are old, and near your punishment; remember.

LEONTIUS
Away base woman.

HIDASPES
Then be no more my Father, but a plague,
I am bound to pray against: be any sin
May force me to despair, and hang my self,

Be thy name never more remembred King
But in example of a broken faith,
And curst even to forgetfulness:
May thy Land bring forth such Monsters as thy Daughter is!
I am weary of my rage. I pray forgive me,
And let me have him, will you Noble Sir?

LEONTIUS
Mercy, mercy heaven:
Thou heir of all dishonor, shamest thou not to draw
This little moisture left for life, thus rudely from me?
Carry that slave to death.

ZOYLUS
For heavens sake Sir, it is no fault of mine,
That she will love me.

LEONTIUS
To death with him, I say.

HIDASPES
Then make haste Tyrant, or I'll be for him:
This is the way to Hell.

LEONTIUS
Hold fast, I charge you away with him.

HIDASPES
Alas old man, Death hath more doors than one,
And I will meet him.

[Exit **HIDASPES**.

LEONTIUS
Dorialus, Pray see her in her chamber,
And lay a guard about her:
The greatest curse the gods lay on our frailties,
Is Will and Disobedience in our Issues,
Which we beget as well as them to plague us,
With our fond loves; Beasts you are only blest
That have that happy dulness to forget
What you have made, your young ones grieve not you
They wander where they list, and have their ways
Without dishonor to you; and their ends,
Fall on 'em without sorrow of their Parents,
Or after ill remembrance: Oh this Woman
Would I had made my self a Sepulcher,
When I made her: Nephew, where is the Prince?

Pray God he have not more part of her baseness
Than of her bloud about him.
Gentlemen, where is he?

ISMENUS
I know not Sir.
H'as his ways by himself, is too wise for my company.

LEONTIUS
I do not like this hiding of himself,
From such society as his person:
Some of it ye needs must know.

ISMENUS
I am sure not I: nor have known twice this ten days, which if I were as proud as some of 'em, I should
take scurvily, but he is a young man. Let him have his swinge, 'twill make him.

[**TIMANTUS** whispers to the **DUKE**.

There's some good matter now in hand:
How the slave jeers and grins; the Duke is pleas'd,
There's a new pair of Scarlet Hose now, and as much
Money to spare, as will fetch the old from pawn,
A Hat and a Cloak to goe out to morrow:
Garters and Stockings come by nature.

LEONTIUS
Be sure of this.

TIMANTUS
I durst not speak else, Sir.

ACTUS SECUNDUS

SCÆNA PRIMA

Cornets. Descend **CUPID**.

CUPID
Leucippus thou art shot through with a shaft
That will not rankle long, yet sharp enough
To sow a world of helpless misery—
In this happie Kingdom, dost thou think
Because thou art a Prince, to make a part
Against my power, but it is all the fault
Of thy old Father, who believes his age

Is cold enough to quench my burning Darts,
But he shall know e'r long, that my smart loose,
Can thaw Ice, and inflame the wither'd heart
Of Nestor, thou thy self art lightly struck,
But his mad love, shall publish that the rage
Of Cupid, has the power to conquer Agenor.

[Exit.

[Enter **BACHA** and **LEUCIPPUS**, **BACHA**, a Handkerchief.

LEUCIPPUS
Why, what's the matter?

BACHA
Have you got the spoil
You thirsted for? Oh tyrannie of men!

LEUCIPPUS
I pray thee leave.

BACHA
Your envy is, Heaven knows,
Beyond the reach of all our feeble sex:
What pain alas, could it have been to you,
If I had kept mine honor? you might still
Have been a Prince, and still this Countreys Heir,
That innocent Guard which I till now had kept,
For my defence, my virtue, did it seem
So dangerous in a State, that your self came to suppress it?

LEUCIPPUS
Drie thine eyes again, I'll kiss thy tears away,
This is but folly, 'tis past all help.

BACHA
Now you have won the treasure,
'Tis my request that you would leave me thus:
And never see these empty Walls again,
I know you will do so, and well you may:
For there is nothing in 'em that's worth
A glance, I loath my self, and am become
Another Woman; One methinks with whom
I want acquaintance.

LEUCIPPUS
If I do offend thee, I can be gone,
And though I love thy sight, so highly do

I prize thine own content, that I will leave thee.

BACHA
Nay, you may stay now;
You should have gone before: I know not now
Why I should fear you: All I should have kept
Is stol'n: Nor is it in the power of man
To rob me farther: if you can invent,
Spare not; No naked man fears robbing less
Than I doe: now you may for ever stay.

LEUCIPPUS
Why, I could do thee farther wrong.

BACHA
You have a deeper reach in evill than I:
'Tis past my thoughts.

LEUCIPPUS
And past my will to act: but trust me I could do it.

BACHA
Good Sir do, that I may know there is a wrong beyond what you have done me.

LEUCIPPUS
I could tell all the world what thou hast done.

BACHA
Yes you may tell the world
And do you think I am so vain to hope
You will not? you can tell the world but this,
That I am a widow, full of tears in shew,
My Husband dead: And one that lov'd me so,
Hardly a week, forgot my modestie,
And caught with youth and greatness,
Gave my self to live in sin with you;
This you may tell: And this I do deserve.

LEUCIPPUS
Why dost thou think me so base to tell!
These limbs of mine shall part
From one another on a wrack,
Ere I disclose; But thou dost utter words
That much afflict me: you did seem as ready
Sweet Bacha, as my self.

BACHA
You are right a man: when they have 'witcht us

into miserie, poor innocent souls,
They lay the fault on us:
But be it so; for Prince Leucippus sake
I will bear any thing.

LEUCIPPUS
Come weep no more,
I wrought thee to it, it was my fault:
Nay, see if thou wilt leave? Here, take this pearl,
Kiss me sweet Bacha, and receive this purse.

BACHA
What should I do with these? they will not
deck my mind.

LEUCIPPUS
Why keep 'em to remember me.
I must be gone, I have been absent long:
I know the Duke my Father is in rage,
But I will see thee suddenly again.
Farewell my Bacha.

BACHA
Gods keep you,
Do you heare Sir: pray give me a point to wear.

LEUCIPPUS
Alas good Bacha, take one, I pray thee where thou wilt.

BACHA
Coming from you. This Point is of as high
Esteem with me, as all pearl and gold:
Nothing but good be ever with or near you.

LEUCIPPUS
Fare thee well mine own good Bacha;
I will make all haste.

[Exit.

BACHA
Just as you are a Dosen I esteem you:
No more, does he think I would prostitute
My self for love? it was the love of these pearls
And gold that won me, I confess
I lust more after him than any other.
And would at any rate if I had store,
Purchase his fellowship: but being poor,

I'll both enjoy his bodie and his purse,
And he a Prince, nere think my self the worse.

[Enter **LEONTIUS, LEUCIPPUS, ISMENUS, TIMANTUS.**

LEONTIUS
Nay, you must back and shew us what it is,
That 'witches you out of your Honor thus.

BACHA
Who's that?

TIMANTUS
Look there Sir.

LEONTIUS
Lady, never flye you are betray'd.

BACHA
Leave me my tears a while,
And to my Just rage give a little place:
What saucy man are you, that without leave,
Enter upon a Widows mournfull house?
You hinder a dead man from many tears.
Who did deserve more than the world can shed,
Though they should weep themselves to Images.
If not for love of me, yet of your self
Away, for you can bring no comfort to me.
But you may carry hence, you know not what.
Nay sorrow is infectious.

LEONTIUS
Thou thy self
Art grown infectious: wouldst thou know my name?
I am the Duke, father to this young-man
Whom thou corrupt'st.

BACHA
Has he then told him all?

LEUCIPPUS
You do her wrong Sir.

BACHA
O he has not told. Sir I beseech you pardon
My wild tongue, directed by a weak distemper'd head
Madded with grief: Alas I did not know
You were my Sovereign; but now you may

Command my poor unworthy life,
Which will be none I hope ere long.

LEONTIUS
All thy dissembling will never hide thy shame:
And wer't not more respecting Womanhood in
General, than any thing in thee, thou shouldst
Be made such an example, that posteritie,
When they would speak most bitterly, should say,
Thou art as impudent as Bacha was.

BACHA
Sir, though you be my King, whom I will
Serve in all just causes: yet when wrongfully
You seek to take my Honor, I will rise
Thus, and defie you; for it is a Jewell
Dearer than you can give, which whilst I keep,
(Though in this lowly house) I shall esteem
My self above the Princes of the earth
That are without it. If the Prince your son,
Whom you accuse me with, know how to speak
Dishonor of me, if he do not do it,
The plagues of hell light on him, may he never
Govern this Kingdome: here I chalenge him
Before the face of heaven, my Liege, and these,
To speak the worst he can: if he will lye,
To lose a womans fame, I'll say he is
Like you (I think I cannot call him worse.)
He's dead, that with his life would have defended
My reputation and I forct to play
(That which I am) the foolish woman,
And use my liberal tongue.

LEUCIPPUS
Is't possible! we men are children in our
Carriages, compar'd with women: 'wake thy self
For shame, and leave not her whose honor thou
Shou'dst keep safe as thine own, alone to free her self:
But I am prest I know not how, with guilt,
And feel my conscience (never us'd to lye)
Loth to allow my tongue to add a lye
To that too much I did: but it is lawfull
To defend her, that only for my Love lov'd evill.

LEONTIUS
Tell me, why did you Leucip: stay here so long?

LEUCIPPUS

If I can urge ought from me but a truth,
Hell take me.

LEONTIUS
What's the matter, why speak you not?

TIMANTUS
Alas good Sir, forbear
To urge the Prince, you see his shamefastness.

BACHA
What does he say Sir? if thou be a Prince
Shew it, and tell the truth.

ISMENUS
If you have lain with her tell your Father
No doubt but he has done as ill before now:
The Gentlewoman will be proud on't.

BACHA
For God's sake speak.

LEUCIPPUS
Have you done prating yet?

ISMENUS
Who prates?

LEUCIPPUS
Thou know'st I do not speak to thee Ismenus:
But what said you Tima; concerning my shamefastness?

TIMANTUS
Nothing I hope that might displease your
Highness.

LEUCIPPUS
If any of thy great, Great-grandmothers
This thousand years, had been as chast as she,
It would have made thee honester, I stay'd
To heare what you wou'd say: she is by heaven
Of the most strict and blameless chastitie
That ever woman was: (good gods forgive me)
Had Tarquin, met with her, she had been kil'd
With a Slave by her ere she had agreed:
I lye with her! wou'd I might perish then.
Our Mothers, whom we all must reverence,
Could nere exceed her for her chastitie,

Upon my soul: for by this light she's
A most obstinate modest creature.

LEONTIUS
What did you with her then so long Leucippus?

LEUCIPPUS
I'll tell you Sir: You see she's beautifull.

LEONTIUS
I see it well.

LEUCIPPUS
Mov'd by her face,
I came with lustful thoughts,
Which was a fault in me:
But telling truth, something more pardonable,
(And for the world I will not lye to you:)
Proud of my self, I thought a Princes name
Had power to blow 'em down flat of their backs;
But here I found a Rock not to be shook:
For as I hope for good Sir, all the battery
That I could lay to her, or of my person,
My greatness, or gold, could nothing move her.

LEONTIUS
'Tis very strange, being so young and fair.

LEUCIPPUS
She's almost thirty Sir.

LEONTIUS
How do you know her age so just?

LEUCIPPUS
She told it me her self
Once when she went about to shew by reason
I should leave wooing her.

LEONTIUS
She stains the ripest Virgins of her age.

LEUCIPPUS
If I had sin'd with her, I would be loth
To publish her disgrace: but by my life
I would have told it you, because I think
You would have pardon'd me the rather:
And I will tell you father: By this light Sir,

(But that I never will bestow my self
But to your liking) if she now would have me,
I now would marry her.

LEONTIUS
How's that Leucippus!

LEUCIPPUS
Sir, will you pardon me one fault, which yet
I have not done, but had a will to do, and I will tell it?

LEONTIUS
Be't what it will I pardon thee.

LEUCIPPUS
I offered marriage to her.

LEONTIUS
Did she refuse it?

LEUCIPPUS
With that earnestness, and almost scorn
To think of any other after her lost Mate, that she
Made me think my self unworthy of her.

LEONTIUS
You have stay'd too long Leucippus.

LEUCIPPUS
Yes Sir, forgive me Heaven, what multitude
Of oaths have I bestow'd on lies, and yet they were
Officious lyes, there was no malice in 'em.

LEONTIUS
She is the fairest creature that ever I beheld;
And then so chaste, 'tis wonderfull: the more I look
On her, the more I am amaz'd.
I have long thought of a wife, and one I would have
Had, but that I was afraid to meet a woman
That might abuse my age: but here she is
Whom I may trust to; of a chastitie
Impregnable, and approved so by my son:
The meaness of her birth will still preserve her
In due obedience; and her beauty is
Of force enough to pull me back to youth.
My son once sent away, whose rivall-ship
I have just cause to fear, if power, or gold,
Or wit, can win her to me, she is mine.

Nephew Ismenus, I have new intelligence,
Your Province is unquiet still.

ISMENUS
Ime glad on't.

LEONTIUS
And so dangerously, that I must send the
Prince in person with you.

ISMENUS
Ime glad of that too: Sir, will you dispatch us
We shall wither here for ever.

LEONTIUS
You shall be dispatcht within this hour:
Leucippus, never wonder, nor ask, it must be thus.
Lady I ask your pardon, whose virtue I have
Slubberd with my tongue, and you shall ever be
Chast in my memory hereafter;
But we old men often doat: to make amends for
My great fault, receive that Ring:
I'm sorry for your grief, may it soon leave you:
Come my Lords lets begon.

[Exeunt.

BACHA
Heaven bless your Grace.
One that had but so much modestie left, as to blush,
Or shrink a little at his first encounter,
Had been undone; where I come off with honor,
And gain too: they that never wou'd be tract
In any course, by the most subtle sense
Must bear it through with frontless impudence.

[Exit.

[Enter **DORIALUS, AGENOR, NISUS**.

DORIALUS
Gentlemen this is a strange peece of Justice,
To put the wretched Dwarf to death because
She doated on him; Is she not a woman, and
Subject to those mad figaries her whole Sex
Is infected with? Had she lov'd you, or you, or I,
Or all on's (as indeed the more the merryer still
With them) must we therefore have our heads par'd

With a Hatchet? So she may love all the Nobility
Out o'th Dukedome in a month, and let the raskals in.

NISUS
You will not, or you do not see the need
That makes this just to the world?

DORIALUS
I cannot tell, I would be loth to feel it:
But the best is, she loves not proper men, we three
Were in wise cases else: but make me know this need.

NISUS
Why yes: He being taken away, this base incontinence dyes presently, and she must see her shame and sorrow for it.

DORIALUS
Pray God she do: but was the Sprat beheaded, Or did they swing him about like a chickin, and so break his neck?

AGENOR
Yes, he was beheaded, and a solemn Justice made of it.

DORIALUS
That might have been deducted.

AGENOR
Why how would you have had him dyed?

DORIALUS
Faith I would have had him rosted like a warden in a brown paper, and no more talk on't: or a feather stuck in's head, like a Quail: or a hanged him in a Dog-coller: what should he be beheaded? we shall have it grow so base shortly, Gentlemen will be out of love with it.

NISUS
I wonder from whence this of the Dwarf's first sprung?

DORIALUS
From an old leacherous pair of breeches that lay upon a wench to keep her warm: for certainly they are no mans work: and I am sure a Monkey would get one of the guard to this fellow, he was no bigger than a small Portmanteu, and much about that making if'tad legs.

AGENOR
But Gentlemen, what say you to the Prince?

NISUS
I, concerning his being sent I know not whither.

DORIALUS

Why then he will come home I know not when: you shall pardon me, I'll talk no more of this subject, but say, gods be with him where ere he is, and send him well home again: For why, he is gone, or when he will return, let them know that directed him: Only this, there's mad Morisco's in the state; but what they are, I'll tell you when I know. Come, let's go, hear all, and say nothing.

AGENOR

Content.

[Exeunt.

[Enter **TIMANTHUS** and **TELAMON**.

TELAMON

Timantus, is the Duke ready yet?

TIMANTUS

Almost.

TELAMON

What ails him?

TIMANTUS

Faith I know not, I think he has dreamt he's but eighteen: has been worse since he sent you forth for the frizling iron.

TELAMON

That cannot be, he lay in Gloves all night, and this morning I brought him a new Periwig, with a lock at it, and knockt up a swing in's chamber.

TIMANTUS

O but since, his Taylor came, and they have fallen out about the fashion on's cloaths: and yonders a fellow come, has board a hole in's ear; and he has bespoke a Vaulting-horse, you shall see him come forth presently: he looks like Winter, stuck here and there with fresh flowers.

TELAMON

Will he not Tilt think you?

TIMANTUS

I think he will.

TELAMON

What does he mean to doe?

TIMANTUS

I know not: but by this light I think he is in love; he wou'd ha' bin shav'd but for me.

TELAMON

In love with whom?

TIMANTUS
I could guess, but you shall pardon me: he will take me along with him some-whither.

TELAMON
I overheard him ask your opinion of some bodies beauty.

TIMANTUS
Yes, there it goes, that makes him so youthfull, and h'as layd by his Crutch, and halts now with a leading staff.

[Enter **LEONTIUS** with a staff and a looking glass.

LEONTIUS
Timantus.

TIMANTUS
Sir.

LEONTIUS
This Feather is not large enough.

TIMANTUS
Yes faith, 'tis such a one as the rest of the young
Gallants wear.

LEONTIUS
Telamon, does it doe well?

TELAMON
Sir, it becomes you, or you become it, the rareliest—

LEONTIUS
Away, dost think so?

TELAMON
Think Sir? I know it. Sir, the Princess, is past all hope of life since the Dwarf was put to death.

LEONTIUS
Let her be so, I have other matters in hand: but this same Taylor angers me, he has made my doublet so wide: and see, the knave has put no points at my arme.

TIMANTUS
Those will be put to quickly Sir, upon any occasion.

LEONTIUS
Telamon, have you bid this Dancer come a mornings?

TELAMON
Yes Sir.

LEONTIUS
Timantus, let me see the glass again: look you how careless you are grown, is this tooth well put in?

TIMANTUS
Which Sir?

LEONTIUS
This Sir.

TIMANTUS
It shall be.

TELAMON
Me thinks that tooth should put him in mind on's years: and Timantus, stands as if (seeing the Duke, in such a youthfull habit) he were looking in's mouth how old he were.

LEONTIUS
So, so,

TELAMON
Will you have your Gown sir?

LEONTIUS
My Gown? why, am I sick? bring me my Sword.

[Exit **TELAMON**.

Timantus,
Let a couple of the great horses be brought out for us.

TIMANTUS
He'll kill himself. Why, will you ride Sir:

LEONTIUS
Ride? Dost thou think I cannot ride?

TIMANTUS
O yes Sir, I know it: but as I conceive your journey, you wou'd have it private; and then you were better take a Coach.

LEONTIUS
These Coaches make me sick: yet 'tis no matter, let it be so.

[Enter **TELAMON** with a sword.

TELAMON
Sir, here's your sword.

LEONTIUS
O well sed: let me see it, I could me thinks
Why Telamon, bring me another: what, thinkst thou
I will wear a sword in vain?

TELAMON
He has not strength enough to draw it,
A yoak of Fleas ty'd to a hair would have drawn it.
'Tis out sir now, the Scabbard is broke.

LEONTIUS
O put it up again, and on with it; me thinks I
am not drest till I feel my sword on.
Telamon, if any of my counsell ask for me,
Say I am gone to take the air.

TIMANTUS
He has not been drest this twenty years then, If
this vain hold but a week, he will learn to play o'th base
violl and sing to't: He's poetical alreadie;
For I have spide a Sonnet on's making lye by's beds side,
I'll be so unmannerly to read it.

[Exit.

[Enter **HIDASPES**, **CLEOPHILA** and **HERO**, **HIDASPES** in a Bed.

HIDASPES
He's dead, he's dead, and I am following.

CLEOPHILA
Ask Cupid mercie Madam.

HIDASPES
O my heart.

CLEOPHILA
Help!

HERO
Stir her:

HIDASPES
O, O!

CLEOPHILA
She's going, wretched women that we are:
Look to her, and I'll pray the while.

HERO
Why Madam?

[She kneels.

CLEOPHILA
Cupid, pardon what is past,
And forgive our sins at last,
Then we will be coy no more,
But thy Deity Adore,
Troths at fifteen we will plight,
And will tread a Dance each night.
In the fields, or by the Fire,
With the youths that have desire.
(How does she yet?)

HERO
O ill:

CLEOPHILA
Given Ear-rings we will wear,
Bracelets of our Lovers hair,
Which they on our Arms shall twist,
With their Names carv'd on our wrist:
All the money that we owe,
We in Tokens will bestow:
And learn to write, that when 'tis sent,
Onely our Loves know what it meant:
O then pardon what is past,
And forgive our Sins at last.
(What, Mends she?)

HERO
Nothing, you do it not wantonly, you shou'd sing.

CLEOPHILA
Why?

HERO
Leave, leave, 'tis now too late.
She is dead: Her last is breathed.

CLEOPHILA

What shall we doe.

HERO
Go run,
And tell the Duke; And whilst I'll close her eyes.
Thus I shut thy faded light,
And put it in eternall night.
Where is she can boldly say
Though she be as fresh as May:
She shall not by this Corps be laid,
Ere to morrows light doe fade.
Let us all now living be,
Warn'd by thy strict Chastitie;
And marry all fast as we can,
Till then we keep a piece of man,
Wrongfully from them that owe it
Soon may every Maid bestow it.

[Exeunt.

[Enter **BACHA** and a **MAID**.

BACHA
Who is it?

MAID
Forsooth there's a gallant Coach at the dore,
And the brave old man in't, that you said was the Duke.

BACHA
Cupid, grant he may be taken. Away:

MAID
He is coming up, and looks the swaggeringst, and has such glorious cloaths.

BACHA
Let all the house see me sad, and see all handsome.

[Enter **LEONTIUS**, and **TIMANTUS**, a Jewell and a Ring.

LEONTIUS
Nay widow flie not back, we come not now to chide, stand up and bid me welcome.

BACHA
To a poor widows house that knows no end of her ill fortune: your Highness is most welcome.

LEONTIUS

Come kiss me then, this is but manners widow: Nere fling your head aside, I have more cause of grief than you: my Daughters dead: but what? 'Tis nothing. Is the rough French horse brought to the dore? They say he is a high goer, I shall soon try his mettle.

TIMANTUS
He will be Sir, and the gray Barbary, they are fiery both.

LEONTIUS
They are the better: Before the gods I am lightsome, very lightsome: How doest thou like me widow?

BACHA
As a person in whom all graces are.

LEONTIUS
Come, come, ye flatter: I'll clap your cheek for that, and you shall not be angry.
Hast no Musick: Now could I cut three times with ease, and do a cross point, should shame all your gallants.

BACHA
I do believe you, and your self too: Lord what a fine old Zany my Love has made him! 'Is mine, I am sure: Heaven make me thankful for him.

LEONTIUS
Tell me how old thou art, my pretty sweet heart?

TIMANTUS
Your Grace will not buy her, she may trip Sir?

BACHA
My sorrow showes me elder then I am by many years.

LEONTIUS
Thou art so witty I must kiss agen.

TIMANTUS
Indeed her Age lyes not in her mouth: nere look it there Sir, she has a better Register, if it be not burnt.

LEONTIUS
I will kiss thee, I am a fire Timantus.

TIMANTUS
Can you chuse Sir, having such heavenly fire before you?

LEONTIUS
Widow, guess why I come, I prethee do.

BACHA

I cannot Sir, unless you be pleas'd to make a mirth out of my rudeness: and that I hope your pity will not let ye, the subject is so Barren: Bite King, Bite, I'll let you play a while.

LEONTIUS
Now as I am an honest man, I'll tell thee truely, how many foot did I Jump yesterday Timantus?

TIMANTUS
Fourteen of your own, and some three fingers.

BACHA
This fellow lyes as lightly, as if hee were in cut Taffata. Alas good Almanack get thee to Bed, and tell what weather we shall have to morrow.

LEONTIUS
Widow I am come in short to be a Suiter.

BACHA
For whom?

LEONTIUS
Why by my troth, I come to wooe thee wench:
And win thee for my self: Nay, look upon me:
I have about me that will do it.

BACHA
Now Heaven defend me, your Whore you shall never: I thank the Gods, I have a little left me to keep me warm, and honest: if your grace take not that, I seek no more.

LEONTIUS
I am so far from taking any thing, I'll add unto thee.

BACHA
Such Additions may be for your ease Sir,
Not my honestie: I am well in being single,
Good Sir seek another, I am no meat for money.

LEONTIUS
Shall I fight for thee?
This sword shall cut his throat, that dars lay claim
But to a Finger of thee, but to a look, I would
See such a fellow.

BACHA
It would be but a cold sight to you:
This is the father of S. George a foot-back,
Can such dry mumming talk.

TIMANTUS

Before the gods, your grace lookes like Æneas.

BACHA
He looks like his old father upon his back,
Crying to get Aboord.

LEONTIUS
How shall I win thy love, I pray thee tell me?
I'll marry thee if thou desirest that: That is an honest
Course, I am in good earnest, and presently within this hour,
I am mad for thee: prethee deny me not,
For as I live I'll pine thee, but I'll have thee.

BACHA
Now he's in the Toyl, I'll hold him fast.

TIMANTUS
You do not know what 'tis to be a Queen,
Go too you Maid, else what the old man falls short of,
There's others can eech out, when you please to call on 'em.

BACHA
I understand you not, Love I adore thee,
Sir, on my knees I give you hearty thanks, for so much
Honoring your humble Hand-mayd above her birth:
Far more her weak deservings, I dare not trust the
Envious tongues of all that must repine at my unworthy rising.
Beside, you have many fair ones in your Kingdome
Born to such worth: O turn your self about
And make a Noble choice.

LEONTIUS
If I do, let me famish: I will have thee,
Or break up house, and boord here.

BACHA
Sir, you may command an unwilling woman to obey ye: but
heaven knows—

LEONTIUS
No more: these half a dozen kisses, and this Jewell, and every thing I have, and away with me, and clap it
up; and have a boy by morning Timantus. let one be sent post for my son again: and for Ismenus, they
are scarce twenty miles on their way yet, by that time we'll be married.

TIMANTUS
There shall Sir.

[Exeunt.

SCÆNA PRIMA

Enter **DORIALUS, AGENOR, NISUS.**

NISUS
Is not this a fine marriage?

AGENOR
Yes, yes, let it alone.

DORIALUS
I, I, the King may marry whom's list, let's talk of other matters.

NISUS
Is the Prince coming home certainly?

DORIALUS
Yes, yes, he was sent post for yesterday, lets make haste we'll see how his new Mother-in-law will entertain him.

NISUS
Why well I warrant you: did you not mark how humbly she carried her self to us on her marriage day, acknowledging her own unworthiness, and that she would be our servant.

DORIALUS
But mark what's done.

NISUS
Regard not shew.

AGENOR
O God! I knew her when I have been off'red her to be brought to my bed for five pound: whether it could have been perform'd or no, I know not.

NISUS
Her Daughters a pretty Lady.

DORIALUS
Yes: and having had but mean bringing up, it talks the pretilest and innocentliest, the Queen will be so angry to hear her betray her breeding by her language: but I am perswaded she's well dispos'd.

AGENOR
I think better than her Mother.

NISUS
Come, we stay too long.

[Exeunt.

[Enter **LEUCIPPUS** and **ISMENUS**.

ISMENUS
How now man, strook dead with a tale?

LEUCIPPUS
No, but with a truth.

ISMENUS
Stand of your self: can you endure blows, and shrink at words?

LEUCIPPUS
Thou knowst I have told thee all.

ISMENUS
But that all's nothing to make you thus: your Sisters dead.

LEUCIPPUS
That's much, but not the most.

ISMENUS
Why, for the other let her marry and hang, 'tis no purpos'd fault of yours: and if your Father will needs have your cast Whore, you shall shew the duty of a child better in being contented, and bidding much good doe his good old heart with her, than in repining thus at it; let her go: what, there are more wenches man, we'll have another.

LEUCIPPUS
O thou art vain, thou knowst I doe not love her:
What shall I doe? I would my tongue had led me
To any other thing, but blasphemy,
So I had mist commending of this woman,
Whom I must reverence now: she is my Mother,
My sin Ismenus has wrought all this ill:
And I beseech thee, to be warn'd by me,
And doe not lye, if any man should aske thee
But How thou dost, or What a clock 'tis now.
Be sure thou doe not lye, make no excuse
For him that is most near thee: never let
The most officious falsehood scape thy tongue,
For they above (that are intirely truth)
Will make that seed, which thou hast sown
Of lyes, yield miseries a thousand fold

Upon thine head, as they have done on mine.

[Enter **TIMANTUS**.

TIMANTUS
Sir, your Highness is welcome home, the Duke and
Queen will presently come forth to you.

LEUCIPPUS
I'll wait on them.

TIMANTUS
Worthy Ismenus, I pray you, have you sped in your wars?

ISMENUS
This Rogue mocks me. Well Timantus, Pray how have you sped here at home at shovelboord?

TIMANTUS
Faith reasonable. How many Towns have you taken in this
Summer?

ISMENUS
How many Stags have you been at the death of this grass?

TIMANTUS
A number: 'Pray how is the Province settled?

ISMENUS
Prethee how does the dun Nag?

TIMANTUS
I think you mock me my Lord.

ISMENUS
Mock thee? Yes by my troth doe I: why what wouldst thou have me doe with thee? Art good for any
thing else?

[Enter **LEONTIUS, BACHA, DORIALUS, AGENOR, NISUS, TELAMON**.

LEUCIPPUS
My good Ismenus, hold me by the wrist:
And if thou see'st me fainting, wring me hard,
For I shall swoon again else.—

[Kneels.

LEONTIUS
Welcome my son; rise, I did send for thee

Back from the province, by thy Mothers counsell,
Thy good Mother here, who loves thee well:
She would not let me venture all my joy
Amongst my enemies: I thank thee for her,
And none but thee, I took her on thy word.

LEUCIPPUS
Pinch harder.

LEONTIUS
And she shall bid thee welcome: I have now
Some near affairs, but I will drink a Health
To thee anon: Come Telamon, Ime grown
Lustier, I thank thee for't, since I marryed;
I can stand now alone, why Telamon,
And never stagger.

[Exit **LEONTIUS, TELAMON.**

BACHA
Welcome most noble Sir, whose fame is come
Hither before your out alas you scorn me,
And teach me what to doe.

LEUCIPPUS
No, you are my Mother.

BACHA
Far unworthy of that name God knows:
But trust me, here before these Lords,
I am no more but Nurse unto the Duke;
Nor will I breed a faction in the State,
It is too much for me that I am rais'd
Unto his bed, and will remain the servant
Of you that did it.

LEUCIPPUS
Madam I will serve you
As shall become me. O dissembling woman!
Whom I must reverence though. Take from thy
Quiver, sure-aim'd Apollo; one of thy swift darts,
Headed with thy consuming golden beams,
And let it melt this body into mist,
That none may find it.

BACHA
Shall I beg my Lords
This Room in private for the Prince and me?

[Exeunt all but **LEUCIPPUS** and **BACHA**.

LEUCIPPUS
What will she say now?

BACHA
I must still enjoy him:
Yet there is still left in me a spark of woman,
That wishes he would move it, but he stands,
As if he grew there with his eyes on earth,
Sir, you and I when we were last together
Kept not this distance as we were afraid
Of blasting by our selves.

LEUCIPPUS
Madam 'tis true, Heaven pardon it.

LEUCIPPUS
Amen Sir.
You may think that I have done you wrong in this strange marriage.

LEUCIPPUS
'Tis past now.

LEUCIPPUS
But it was no fault of mine:
The world had call'd me mad, had I refus'd
The King: nor layd I any train to catch him,
It was your own Oaths did it.

LEUCIPPUS
'Tis a truth: that takes my sleep away, but
Would to Heaven, if it had so been pleas'd, you had
Refus'd him, though I had gratifi'd that courtesie
With having you my self: But since 'tis thus,
I doe beseech you that you will be honest
From henceforth; and not abuse his credulous Age,
Which you may easily doe. As for my self
What I can say, you know alas too well
Is ty'd within me, here it will sit like lead,
But shall offend no other, it will pluck me
Back from my ent'rance into any mirth,
As if a servant came, and whisper'd with me
Of some friends death, but I will bear my self,
To you, with all the due obedience
A son owes to a Mother: more than this,
Is not in me, but I must leave the rest to the

Just gods: who in their blessed time,
When they have given me punishment enough,
For my rash Sin, will mercifully find
As unexpected means to ease my grief
As they did now to bring it.

BACHA
Grown so godly? this must not be.
And I will be to you, no other than a natural Mother ought;
And for my honesty, so you will swear
Never to urge me, I shall keep it safe from any other.

LEUCIPPUS
Bless me I should urge you?

BACHA
Nay but swear then that I may be at peace,
For I doe feel a weakness in my self,
That can denie you nothing, if you tempt me,
I shall embrace Sin as it were a friend, and run to meet it.

LEUCIPPUS
If you knew how far
It were from me, you would not urge an Oath.
But for your satisfaction, when I tempt you.

BACHA
Swear not: I cannot move him, this sad talk
Of things past help, does not become us well.
Shall I send one for my Musicians, and we'll dance?

LEUCIPPUS
Dance Madam?

BACHA
Yes, Alavalta.

LEUCIPPUS
I cannot dance Madam.

BACHA
Then lets be merry.

LEUCIPPUS
I am as my Fortunes bid me.
Do not you see me sowr?

BACHA

Yes.
And why think you I smile?

LEUCIPPUS
I am so far from any joy my self,
I cannot fancie a cause of mirth.

BACHA
I'll tell you, we are alone:

LEUCIPPUS
Alone?

BACHA
Yes.

LEUCIPPUS
'Tis true: what then?

BACHA
What then? you make my smiling now
Break into laughter: what think you Is to be done then?

LEUCIPPUS
We shou'd pray to Heaven for mercy.

BACHA
Pray? that were a way indeed
To pass the time: but I will make you blush,
To see a bashfull woman teach a man
What we should doe alone: try again
If you can find it out.

LEUCIPPUS
I dare not think I understand you.

BACHA
I must teach you then; Come, kiss me.

LEUCIPPUS
Kiss you?

BACHA
Yes, be not asham'd:
You did it not your self, I will forgive you.

LEUCIPPUS
Keep you displeas'd gods, the due respect

I ought to bear unto this wicked woman,
As she is now my Mother, Haste within me,
Lest I add sins to sins, till no repentance will cure me.

BACHA
Leave these melancholly moods,
That I may swear thee welcome on thy Lipps
A thousand times.

LEUCIPPUS
Pray leave this wicked talk,
You doe not know to what my Fathers wrong
May urge me.

BACHA
I'm careless, and doe weigh
The world, my life, and all my after hopes
Nothing without thy Love, mistake me not:
Thy Love, as I have had it, free and open
As wedlock is, within it self, what say you?

LEUCIPPUS
Nothing.

BACHA
Pitty me, behold a Duchess
Kneels for thy mercie, and I swear to you
Though I should lye with you, it is no Lust,
For it desires no change, I could with you
Content my self; what answer will you give?

LEUCIPPUS
They that can answer must be less amaz'd,
Than I am now: you see my tears deliver
My meaning to you.

BACHA
Shall I be contem'd? thou art a beast, worse than a savage beast,
To let a Lady kneel, to beg that thing
Which a right man would offer.

LEUCIPPUS
'Tis your will Heaven: but let me bear me like
My self, how ever she does.

BACHA
Were you made an Eunuch, since you went hence?
Yet they have more desire than I can find in you:

How fond was I to beg thy love! I'll force thee to my will
Dost thou not know that I can make the King
Dote as my list? yield quickly, or by Heaven
I'll have thee kept in prison for my purpose,
Where I will make thee serve my turn, and have thee fed
With such meats as best shall fit my ends
And not thy health, why dost not speak to me?
And when thou dost displease me, and art grown
Less able to perform; then I will have thee
Kill'd and forgotten: Are you striken dumb?

LEUCIPPUS
All you have nam'd but making of me sin
With you, you may command, but never that;
Say what you will, I'll hear you as becomes me,
If you speak, I will not follow your counsell,
Neither will I tell the world to your disgrace,
But give you the just honor
That is due from me to my Father's wife.

BACHA
Lord how full of wise formality you are grown
Of late: but you were telling me
You could have wisht that I had marry'd you,
If you will swear so yet, I'll make away the King.

LEUCIPPUS
You are a strumpet.

BACHA
Nay, I care not
For all your Railings: They will Batter walls
And take in Towns, as soon as trouble me:
Tell him, I care not, I shall undoe you only, which is no matter.

LEUCIPPUS
I appeal to you still, and for ever, that are
And cannot be other, Madam, I see 'tis in your power
To work your will on him: And I desire you
To lay what trains you will for my wish'd death,
But suffer him to find his quiet grave
In peace; Alas he never did you wrong,
And farther I beseech you pardon me,
For the ill word I gave you, for how ever
You may deserve, it became not me
To call you so, but passion urges me
I know not whither: my heart break now, & ease me ever.

BACHA
Pray you get you hence
With your goodly humor, I am weary of you extreamely:

LEUCIPPUS
Trust me, so am I of my self too:
Madam, I'll take my leave; gods set all right.

BACHA
Amen, Sir, get you gon;
Am I deny'd? it does not trouble me
That I have mov'd, but that I am refus'd:
I have lost my patience: I will make him know
Lust is not Love, for Lust will find a mate
While there are men, and so will I: and more

[Enter **TIMANTUS**.

Than one, or twenty: yonder is Timantus,
A fellow void of any worth, to raise himself,
And therefore like to catch at any evil
That will but pluck him up: him will I make
Mine own: Timantus.

TIMANTUS
Madam?

BACHA
Thou know'st well
Thou wert by chance, a means of this my raising:
Brought the Duke to me, and though 'twere but chance
I must reward thee.

TIMANTUS
I shall bend my service unto your Highness.

BACHA
But do it then entirely, and in every thing,
And tell me, couldst thou now think that thing
Thou wouldst not do for me?

TIMANTUS
No by my soul Madam.

BACHA
Then thou art right.
Go to my Lodging, and I'll follow thee.

[Exit **TIMANTUS**.

With my instruction I do see already,
This Prince that did but now contemn me, dead:
Yet will I never speak an evil word
Unto his Father of him, till I have won
A belief, I love him, but I'll make
His virtues his undoing, and my praises
Shall be so many swords against his breast,
Which once perform'd, I'll make Urania
My Daughter, the Kings heir, and plant my issue
In this large Throne: nor shall it be withstood,
They that begin in Lust, must end in Blood.

[Exit.

[Enter **DORIALUS, AGENOR, NISUS**.

DORIALUS
We live to know a fine time, Gentl.

NISUS
And a fine Duke, that through his doting age
Suffers him to be a child again
Under his Wives tuition.

AGENOR
All the Land holds in that tenor too: in womans
service? sure we shall learn to spinn.

DORIALUS
No, that's too honest: we shall have other
Liberal Sciences taught us too soon;
Lying, and flattering, those are the studies now:
And Murther shortly I know, will be humanity, Gent.
If we live here we must be knaves, believe it.

NISUS
I cannot tell my Lord Dorialus, though my
Own nature hate it, if all determine to be knaves,
I'll try what I can do upon my self: that's certain,
I will not have my throat cut for my goodness,
The virtue will not quit the pain.

AGENOR
But pray you tell me,
Why is the Prince, now ripe and full experient,
Not made a dore in the State?

NISUS
Because he is honest.

[Enter **TIMANTUS**.

TIMANTUS
Goodness attend your Honors.

DORIALUS
You must not be amongst us then.

TIMANTUS
The Dutchess, whose humble servant I am proud to be, would speak with you.

AGENOR
Sir, we are pleas'd to wait: when is it?

TIMANTUS
An hour hence my good Lords, and so I leave my service.

DORIALUS
This is one of her Ferrets that she bolts business out withall: this fellow, if he were well ript, has all the linings of a knave within him: how slye he looks!

NISUS
Have we nothing about our cloaths that he may catch at?

AGENOR
O my conscience, there's no treason in my dublet, if there be, my elbows will discover it, they are out.

DORIALUS
Faith, and all the harm that I can find in mine is, that they are not pay'd for; let him make what he can of that, so he discharge that. Come, let's go.

[Exeunt.

[Enter **BACHA, LEONTIUS, TELLAMON**.

BACHA
And you shall find Sir what a blessing heaven gave you in such a son.

LEONTIUS
Pray gods, I may, Let's walk & change our subject.

BACHA
O Sir, can any thing come sweeter to you, or strike a deeper joy into your heart than your son's virtue?

LEONTIUS
I allow his virtues: but 'tis not handsome thus to feed my self with such moderate praises of mine own.

BACHA
The subject of our comendations is it self grown so infinite in goodness, that all the glory we can lay upon it, though we should open volumes of his praises, is a mere modesty in his expression, and shews him lame still, like an ill wrought peece wanting proportion.

LEONTIUS
Yet still he is a man, and subject still to more inordinate vices, than our love can give him blessing.

BACHA
Else he were a god: yet so near as he is, he comes to heaven, that we may see so far as flesh can point us things only worthy them, and only these in all his actions.

LEONTIUS
This is too much my Queen.

LEUCIPPUS
Had the gods lov'd me; that my unworthy womb had bred this brave man.

LEONTIUS
Still you run wrong.

LEUCIPPUS
I would have liv'd upon the comfort of him; fed on his growing hopes.

LEONTIUS
This touches me.

LEUCIPPUS
I know no friends, nor Being, but his virtues.

LEONTIUS
You have laid out words enough upon a subject.

LEUCIPPUS
But words cannot express him Sir: why what a shape
Heaven has conceiv'd him in, oh Nature made him up!

LEONTIUS
I wonder Dutchess.

LEUCIPPUS
So you must: for less than admiration loses this godlike man.

LEONTIUS
Have you done with him?

LEUCIPPUS
Done with? O good gods what frailties thus pass by us without reverence!

LEONTIUS
I see no such perfection.

BACHA
O dear Sir: you are a father, and those joys
To you, speak in your heart, not in your tongue.

LEONTIUS
This leaves a tast behind it worse than physick.

BACHA
Then for all his wisdome, valour,
Good fortune, and all those friends of honor,
They are in him as free and natural, as passions
In a Woman.

LEONTIUS
You make me blush at all these years
To see how blindly you have flung your praises
Upon a Boy, a very child, and worthless,
Whilst I live, of these Honors.

BACHA
I would not have my love Sir, make my tongue
Shew me so much a woman: as to praise
Or dispraise, where my will is, without reason,
Or generall allowance of the people.

LEONTIUS
Allowance of the people, what allow they?

BACHA
All, I have sed for truth, and they must do it,
And doat upon him: love him, and admire him.

LEONTIUS
How's that?

BACHA
For in this youth and noble forwardness
All things are bound together that are kingly,
A fitness to bear rule:

LEONTIUS

No more.

BACHA
And Sovereignty not made to know command.

LEONTIUS
I have sed, no more.

BACHA
I have done Sir, though unwilling, and pardon me.

LEONTIUS
I do, not a word more.

BACHA
I have gi'n thee poyson
Of more infection than the Dragons tooth,
Or the gross Air o'er heated.

LEONTIUS
Timantus when saw you the Prince?

TIMANTUS
I left him now Sir.

LEONTIUS
Tell me truely, out of your free opinion without courting. How you like him.

TIMANTUS
How I like him?

LEONTIUS
Yes: for you in conversation may see more
Than a Father.

BACHA
It works.

TIMANTUS
Your Grace has chosen out an ill observer.

LEONTIUS
Yes, I mean of his ill: you talk rightly.

TIMANTUS
But you take me wrong: All I know by him
I dare deliver boldly: He is the storehouse
And head of virtue; your great self excepted,

That feeds the Kingdome.

LEONTIUS
These are flatteries: speak me his vices, there you do a service worth a Fathers thanks.

TIMANTUS
Sir, I cannot. If there be any, sure they are the times which I could wish less dangerous. But pardon me, I am too bold.

LEONTIUS
You are not, forward and open what these dangers are.

TIMANTUS
Nay, good Sir.

LEONTIUS
Nay, fall not off again, I will have all.

TIMANTUS
Alas Sir, what am I, you should believe
My eyes or ears, so subtle to observe
Faults in a State: all my main business
Is service to your Grace, and necessaries
For my poor life.

LEONTIUS
Do not displease me Sirrah,
But that you know tell me, and presently.

TIMANTUS
Since your Grace will have it
I'll speak it freely: Alwayes my obedience
And love preserv'd unto the Prince.

LEONTIUS
Prethee to the matter.

TIMANTUS
For Sir, if you consider
How like a Sun in all his great employments,
How full of heat.

LEONTIUS
Make me understand what I desire.

TIMANTUS
And then at his return.

LEONTIUS
Do not anger me.

TIMANTUS
Then thus Sir: All mislike ye,
As they would do the gods, if they did dwell with 'em.

LEONTIUS
What?

TIMANTUS
Talke and prate, as their ignorant rages
Leads 'em without Alleageance or Religion.
For Heavens sake have a care of your own person:
I cannot tell, their wickedness may lead
Farther than I dare think yet.

LEONTIUS
O base people.

TIMANTUS
Yet the Prince, for whom this is pretended may
Persuade 'em, and no doubt will: virtue is ever watchfull,
But be you still secur'd and comforted.

LEONTIUS
Heaven how have I offended, that this rod
So heavy and unnaturall, should fall upon me
When I am old and helpless.

TIMANTUS
Brave Gentl. that such a madding love should follow
thee, to rob thee of a Father:
All the Court is full of dangerous whispers.

LEONTIUS
I perceive it, and 'spight of all their strengths
Will make my safety: I'll cut him shorter.
I'll cut him shorter first, then let him rule.

LEUCIPPUS
What a foul Age is this, when Virtue is made a
sword to smite the virtuous! Alas, alas:

LEONTIUS
I'll teach him to fly lower.

TIMANTUS

By no means Sir, rather, make more your love,
And hold your favor to him: for 'tis now
Impossible to yoke him, if his thoughts,
As I must ne'er believe, run with their rages,
He never was so innocent, but what reason
His Grace has to withdraw his love from me,
And other good men that are near your person,
I cannot yet find out: I know my duty
Has ever been attending.

LEONTIUS
'Tis too plain: He means to play the villain,
I'll prevent him, not a word more of this, be private.

[Exit **LEONTIUS**.

TIMANTUS
Madam 'tis done.

BACHA
He cannot escape me. Have you spoken with the noble men?

TIMANTUS
Yes Madam they are here: I wait a farther service.

BACHA
Till you see the Prince, you need no more instructions.

TIMANTUS
No, I have it.

[Exit **TIMANTUS**.

[Enter **DORIALUS, NISUS, AGENOR**.

BACHA
That fool that willingly provoks a woman,
Has made himself another evill Angell,
And a new Hell, to which all other tormentes
Are but mere pastime: Now my noble Lords,
You must excuse me, that unmannerly
We have broke your private business.

AGENOR
Your good Grace may command us, and that.

BACHA
Faith my Lord Agenor: 'Tis so good a cause

I am confident, you cannot loose by it.

DORIALUS
Which way does she fish now?
The devill is but a fool to a right woman.

NISUS
Madam, we must needs win in doing service to such a gracious Lady.

BACHA
I thank you, and will let you know the business:
So I may have your helps, never be doubtfull,
For 'tis so just a cause, and will to you
Upon the knowledge seem so honorable,
That I assure my self your willing hearts
Will strait be for me in it.

AGENOR
If she should prove good now, what wer't like?

DORIALUS
Thunder in Januarie, or a good woman,
That's stranger than all Affrick.

BACHA
It shall not need your wonder, this it is:
The Duke you know is old, and rather subject
To ease and prayers now, than all those troubles,
Cares, and continuall watchings, that attend
A Kingdomes safety, therefore to prevent
The fall of such a flourishing Estate
As this has ever been, and to put off
The murmure of the people that encrease
Against my government, which the gods knows
I onely feel the trouble of: I present
The Prince unto your loves, a Gent.
In whom all Excellencies are knit together,
All peeces of a true man, let your prayers
Win from the Duke half his Vexation,
That he may undertake it, whose discretion
I must confess, though it be from the Father,
Yet now is stronger, and more apt to govern.
'Tis not my own desire, but all the Lands,
I know the weakeness of it.

NISUS
Madam, this noble care and love has won us
For ever to your lives, we'll to the King,

And since your Grace has put it in our mouths,
We'll win him with the cunning'st words we can.

DORIALUS
I was never cousen'd in a woman before.
For commonly they are like Apples: If once they bruise
They will grow rotten thorow, and serve for nothing but to
asswage swellings.

BACHA
Good Lords delay no time, since 'tis your good
Pleasures to think my counsell good, and by no means
Let the Prince know it, whose affections
Will stir mainly against it: besides his Father
May hold him dangerous, if it be not carried
So that his forward will appear not in it,
Go, and be happy.

DORIALUS
Well, I would not be Chronicl'd as thou
Wilt be for a good woman, for all the world.

NISUS
Madam, we kiss your hand, and so inspire.
Nothing but happiness can crown our prayers.

[Exeunt.

ACTUS QUARTUS

SCÆNA PRIMA

Enter **LEUCIPPUS, ISMENUS.**

LEUCIPPUS
And thus she has us'd me, is't not a good mother?

ISMENUS
Why kill'd you her not?

LEUCIPPUS
The gods forbid it.

ISMENUS
S'light, if all the women i'th' world were barren, shee had dy'd.

LEUCIPPUS
But 'tis not reason directs thee thus.

ISMENUS
Then have I none at all, for all I have in me
Directs me: Your Father's in a pretty rage.

LEUCIPPUS
Why?

ISMENUS
Nay, 'tis well, if he know himself, but some of the Nobility have deliver'd a petition to him: what's in't, I know not, but it has put him to his trumps: he has taken a months time to answer it, and chafes like himself.

[Enter **LEONTIUS**, **BACHA** and **TELLAMON**.

LEUCIPPUS
He's here Ismenus.

LEONTIUS
Set me down Tellamon. Leucippus.

LEUCIPPUS
Sir.

LEUCIPPUS
Nay good Sir, be at peace, I dare swear he knew not of it.

LEONTIUS
You are foolish: peace.

LEUCIPPUS
All will go ill, deny it boldly Sir, trust me he cannot prove it by you.

LEUCIPPUS
What?

LEUCIPPUS
You'll make all worse too with your facing it.

LEUCIPPUS
What is the matter?

LEONTIUS
Know'st thou that petition?
Look on it well: wouldst thou be joyn'd with me
(Unnaturall child to be weary of me)

E'r Fate esteem me fit for other worlds.

BACHA
May be he knows not of it.

LEUCIPPUS
Oh strange carriages!
Sir, as I have hope that there is any thing
To reward doing well, my usages
Which have been (but 'tis no matter what)
Have put me so far from the thought of Greatness,
That I should welcome it like a disease
That grew upon me, and I could not cure.
They are my enemies that gave you this,
And yet they call me friend, and are themselves
I fear abus'd. I am weary of my life,
For Gods sake take it from me: it creates
More mischief in the State than it is worth,
The usage I have had, I know would make
Wisdom her self run frantick through the streets,
And Patience quarrel with her shadow.
Sir, this sword—

BACHA
Alas! help for the love of Heaven,
Make way through me first, for he is your Father.

LEONTIUS
What, would he kill me?

BACHA
No Sir, no.

LEONTIUS
Thou always mak'st the best on't, but I fear—

LEUCIPPUS
Why do you use me thus? who is't can think
That I would kill my Father, that can yet
Forbear to kill you? Here Sir, is my sword;
I dare not touch it, lest she say again
I would have kill'd you: let me not have mercy
When I most need it, if I would not change
Place with my meanest servant. Let these faults
Be mended Madam: if you saw how ill
They did become you, you would part with them.

BACHA

I told the Duke as much before.

LEUCIPPUS
What? what did you tell him?

BACHA
That it was only an ambition,
Nurst in you by your youth, provok'd you thus,
Which age would take away.

LEONTIUS
It was his doing then? come hither Love.

BACHA
No indeed, Sir.

LEUCIPPUS
How am I made, that I can bear all this?
If any one had us'd a friend of mine nere this,
My hand had carried death about it.

LEONTIUS
Lead me hence Tellamon: come my dear
Bacha, I shall find time for this.

ISMENUS
Madam, you know I dare not speak before
The King; but you know well, if not, I'll tell it you,
You are the most wicked'st, and most murderous
Strumpet, that ever was call'd Woman.

BACHA
My Lord, what can I do for him? he shall command me.

LEONTIUS
I know thou art too kind; away I say.

[Exit **LEONTIUS**, **BACHA**, **TIMANTUS** and **TELLAMON**.

ISMENUS
Sir, I am sure we dream, this cannot be.

LEUCIPPUS
Oh that we did, my wickedness has brought
All this to pass, else I should bear my self.

[Enter **URANIA**.

ISMENUS

Look, doe you see who's there? your virtuous Mothers issue: kill her, yet take some little pidling revenge.

LEUCIPPUS

Away, the whole Court calls her virtuous; for they say, she is unlike her Mother, and if so, she can have no vice.

ISMENUS

I'll trust none of 'em that come of such a breed.

LEUCIPPUS

But I have found
A kind of love in her to me: alas,
Think of her death! I dare be sworn for her,
She is as free from any hate to me
As her bad Mother's full. She was brought up
I'th' Countrey, as her tongue will let you know

If you but talk with her, with a poor Uncle,
Such as her Mother had.

ISMENUS

She's come again.

URANIA

I would fene speak to the good Marquess my brother, if I but thought he could abaid me.

LEUCIPPUS

Sister, how do you?

URANIA

Very well I thank you.

ISMENUS

How does your good Mother?

LEUCIPPUS

Fie, fie, Ismenus for shame, mock such an innocent soul as this.

URANIA

Feth a she be no good, God may her so.

LEUCIPPUS

I know you wish it with your heart dear Sister, but she is good I hope.

ISMENUS

Are you so simple, to make so much of this?

Do you not know,
That all her wicked Mother labours for, is but to raise
Her to your right, and leave her this Dukedom?

URANIA
I, but ne'r Sir be afred;
For though she take th' ungain'st weas she can,
I'll ne'er ha't fro' you.

LEUCIPPUS
I should hate my self Ismenus;
If I should think of her simplicity,
Ought but extreamly well.

ISMENUS
Nay, as you will.

URANIA
And though she be my Mother,
If she take any caurse to do you wrong,
If I can see't, youst quickly hear on't Sir:
And so I'll take my leave.

LEUCIPPUS
Farewel good Sister, I thank you.

[Exit **URANIA**.

ISMENUS
You believe all this.

LEUCIPPUS
Yes.

[Enter **TIMANTUS**.

ISMENUS
A good faith doth well, but methinks
It were no hard matter now, for her Mother to send her:
Yonder's one you may trust if you will too.

LEUCIPPUS
So I will, if he can shew me as apparent signs
Of truth as she did; Does he weep Ismenus?

ISMENUS
Yes, I think so: some good's happen'd I warrant:
Do you hear, you? What honest man has scap'd misery,

That you are crying thus?

TIMANTUS
Noble Ismenus, where's the Prince?

ISMENUS
Why there! hast wept thine eyes out?

TIMANTUS
Sir, I beseech you hear me.

LEUCIPPUS
Well, speak on.

ISMENUS
Why, will you hear him?

LEUCIPPUS
Yes Ismenus, why?

ISMENUS
I would hear blasphemy as willingly.

LEUCIPPUS
You are to blame.

TIMANTUS
No Sir: he is not to blame:
If I were as I was.

ISMENUS
Nor as thou art, yfaith awhit to blame.

LEUCIPPUS
What's your business?

TIMANTUS
Faith Sir, I am ashamed to speak before you,
My conscience tells me I have injur'd you,
And by the earnest instigation
Of others, have not done you to the King
Always the best and friendliest offices;
Which pardon me, or I will never speak.

ISMENUS
Never pardon him and silence a knave.

LEUCIPPUS

I pardon thee.

TIMANTUS
Your Mother sure is naught.

LEUCIPPUS
Why shouldst thou think so?

TIMANTUS
Oh noble, Sir, your honest eyes perceive not
The dangers you are led to; shame upon her,
And what fell miseries the gods can think on
Shower down upon her wicked head, she has plotted
I know too well your death: would my poor life
Or thousands such as mine is, might be offer'd
Like sacrifices up for your preserving,
What free oblations would she have to glut her,
But she is merciless, and bent to ruin;
If heaven and good men step not to your rescue,
And timely, very timely: Oh this Dukedom!
I weep, I weep for the poor Orphans i'th' Countrey
Left with but Friends or Parents.

LEUCIPPUS
Now Ismenus, what think you of this fellow?
This was a lying knave, a flatterer,
Does not this Love still shew him so.

ISMENUS
This Love? this Halter: if he prove not yet
The cunning'st rankest rogue that ever Canted,
I'll never see man again: I know him to bring,
And can interpret every new face he makes;
Look how he wrings like a good stool for a tear:
Take heed, Children and Fools
First feel the smart, Then weep.

LEUCIPPUS
Away, away, such an unkind distrust,
Is worse than a dissembling, if it be one,
And sooner leads to mischief, I believe it,
And him an honest man: he could not carry
Under an evil cause, so true a sorrow.

ISMENUS
Take heed, this is your Mothers scorpion,
That carries stings even in his tears,
Whose soul is a rank poison through: Touch

Not at him, if you do, you are gone, if you had twenty
Lives: I knew him for a Roguish boy, when
He would poison Dogs, and keep tame Toads,
He lay with his Mother, and infected her, and now
She begs i'th' Hospital, with a patch of Velvet,
Where her Nose stood: like the Queen of Spades.
And all her teeth in her purse, the Devil and this
Fellow are so near, 'Tis not yet known which is the eviler Angel.

LEUCIPPUS

Nay, then I see 'tis spite: Come hither friend.
Hast thou not heard the cause yet that incens'd my Mother
to my death, for I protest I feel none in my self?

TIMANTUS

Her Will Sir, and Ambition, as I think,
Are the provokers of it, as in Women,
Those two are ever powerful to destruction,
Beside a hate of your still growing virtues,
She being only wicked.

LEUCIPPUS

Heavens defend me as I am innocent,
And ever have been from all immoderate thoughts and
Actions, that carry such rewards along with 'em.

TIMANTUS

Sir, all I know, my duty must reveal,
My Countrey and my Love command it from me,
For whom I'll lay my life down: this night coming,
A Counsel is appointed by the Duke,
To sit about your apprehension:
If you dare trust my faith: which by all good things
Shall ever watch about you: goe along,
And to a place I'll guide you: where no word
Shall scape without your hearing, nor no plot
Without discovering to you, which once known,
You have your answers and prevention.

ISMENUS

You are not so mad to goe; shift off this fellow, you shall be rul'd once by a wise man: Ratsbane get you gone, or—

LEUCIPPUS

Peace, peace for shame, thy love is too suspitious, 'tis a way offer'd to preserve my life, and I will take it: be my Guide Timantus and do not mind this angry man, thou know'st him: I may live to requite thee.

TIMANTUS

Sir, this service is done for virtues sake, not for reward, however he may hold me.

ISMENUS

The great pox on you: but thou hast that curse so much, 'twill grow a blessing in thee shortly. Sir, for wisdoms sake court not your death, I am your friend and subject, and I shall lose in both: if I lov'd you not, I would laugh at you, and see you run your neck into the noose, and cry a Woodcock.

LEUCIPPUS

So much of man, and so much fearful; fie, prethee have peace within thee: I shall live yet many a golden day to hold thee here dearest and nearest to me: Go on Timantus, I charge you by your love no more, no more.

[Exeunt **LEUCIPPUS and TIMANTUS.**

ISMENUS

Goe, and let your own rod whip you:
I pity you. And dog, if he miscarry thou shalt pay for't,
I'll study for thy punishment, and it shall last
Longer and sharper than a tedious Winter,
Till thou blasphem'st, and then thou diest and damn'st.

[Exit.

[Enter **LEONTIUS** and **TELLAMON.**

LEONTIUS

I wonder the Dutchess comes not.

TELLAMON

She has heard, Sir, your Will to speak with her:
But there is something leaden at her heart;
(Pray God it be not mortal) that even keeps her
From conversation with her self.

[Enter the **DUTCHESS.**

BACHA

Oh whither will you my cross affections pull me?
Fortune, Fate, and you whose powers direct our actions,
And dwell within us: you that are Angels
Guiding to virtue, wherefore have you given
So strong a hand to evil? wherefore suffer'd
A Temple of your own, you Deities
Where your fair selves dwelt only, and your goodness
Thus to be soyl'd with sin?

LEONTIUS

Heaven bless us all.

From whence comes this distemper? speak my fair one.

BACHA
And have you none, Love and Obedience,
Your ever faithful Servants to imploy
In this strange story of impiety,
But me a Mother; Must I be your strumpet?
To lay black Treason upon, and in him,
In whom all sweetness was: in whom my love
Was proud to have a Being, in whom Justice,
And all the gods for our imaginations
Can work into a man, were more than virtues,
Ambition down to hell, where thou wert foster'd,
Thou hast poison'd the best soul, the purest, whitest,
And meerest innocent'st it self that ever
Mens greedy hopes gave life to.

LEONTIUS
This is still stranger: lay this treason
Open to my correction.

BACHA
Oh what a combat duty and affection
Breeds in my blood!

LEONTIUS
If thou conceal'st him, may,
Beside my death, the curses of the Countrey,
Troubles of conscience, and a wretched end,
Bring thee unto a poor forgotten grave.

LEUCIPPUS
My Being: for another tongue to tell it,
Cease, a Mother! some good man that dares
Speak for his King and Countrey: I am full
Of too much womans pity: yet oh Heaven,
Since it concerns the safety of my Sovereign,
Let it not be a cruelty in me,
Nor draw a Mothers name in question,
Amongst unborn people, to give up that man
To Law and Justice, that unrighteously
Has sought his Fathers death: be deaf: be deaf Sir,
Your Son is the offender: Now have you all,
Would I might never speak again.

LEONTIUS
My Son! Heaven help me.
No more! I thought it, and since

His life is grown so dangerous: Let them that
Gave him, take him: he shall dye,
And with him all my fears.

BACHA
Oh use your mercy: you have a brave subject
To bestow it on. I'll forgive him, Sir; and for his
Wrong to me, I'll be before ye.

LEONTIUS
Durst his villany extend to thee?

BACHA
Nothing but heats of youth, Sir.

LEONTIUS
Upon my life he sought my bed.

BACHA
I must confess he loved me
Somewhat beyond a Son: and still pursu'd it
With such a Lust, I will not say Ambition:
That clean forgetting all obedience,
And only following his first heat unto me,
He hotly sought your death, and me in Marriage.

LEONTIUS
Oh Villain!

BACHA
But I forget all: and am half asham'd
To press a man so far.

[Enter **TIMANTUS**.

TIMANTUS
Where is the Duke? for Gods sake bring me to him:

LEONTIUS
Here I am: each corner of the Dukedom
Sends new affrights forth: what wouldst thou? speak.

TIMANTUS
I cannot Sir, my fear ties up my tongue:

LEONTIUS
Why, what's the matter? Take thy courage
To thee, and boldly speak, where are the Guard?

In the gods name, out with it:

TIMANTUS
Treason, treason.

LEONTIUS
In whom?

BACHA
Double the Guard.

TIMANTUS
There is a fellow, Sir.

LEONTIUS
Leave shaking man.

TIMANTUS
'Tis not for fear, but wonder.

LEONTIUS
Well

TIMANTUS
There is a fellow, Sir, close i'th' Lobby:
You o'the Guard, look to the door there.

LEONTIUS
But let me know the business.

TIMANTUS
Oh that the hearts of men should be so hard'ned
Against so good a Duke, for Gods sake, Sir,
Seek means to save your self; This wretched slave
Has his sword in his hand, I know his heart:
Oh it hath almost kill'd me with the thought of it.

LEONTIUS
Where is he?

[Enter the **GUARD** and bring him in.

TIMANTUS
I'th' Lobby Sir, close in a corner:
Look to your selves for Heavens sake,
Me thinks he is here already.
Fellows of the Guard be valiant.

LEONTIUS
Goe Sirs, and apprehend him; Treason shall
Never dare me in mine own Gates.

TIMANTUS
'Tis done.

[There they bring the **PRINCE** in.

BACHA
And thou shalt find it to thy best content.

LEONTIUS
Are these the comforts of my age?
They're happy that end their daies contented
With a little, and live aloof from dangers, to a King
Every content doth a new peril bring.
Oh let me live no longer, shame of Nature,
Bastard to Honor: Traytor, Murderer,
Devil in a humane shape. Away with him,
He shall not breathe his hot infection here.

LEUCIPPUS
Sir, hear me.

LEONTIUS
Am I or he your Duke? away with him
To a close prison: your Highness now shall know,
Such branches must be cropt before they grow.

LEUCIPPUS
Whatever fortune comes, I bid it welcome,
My innocency is my Armor: gods preserve you.

[Exit.

BACHA
Fare thee well, I shall never see so brave a Gent.
Would I could weep out his offences.

TIMANTUS
Or I could weep out mine eyes.

LEONTIUS
Come Gentlemen, we'll determine presently
About his death: we cannot be too forward in our
Safety: I am very sick, lead me unto my bed.

[Exeunt.

[Enter **1ST CITIZEN** and his **BOY**.

1ST CITIZEN
Sirrah, goe fetch my Fox from the Cutlers: There's money for the scowring: Tell him I stop a groat since the last great Muster: he had in stone Pitch for the bruise: he took with the recoyling of his Gun.

BOY
Yes Sir.

1ST CITIZEN
And do you hear? when you come, Take down my Buckler, and sweep the Cobwebs off: and grind the pick on't, and fetch a Nail or two: and tack on bracers: your Mistriss made a pot-lid ont't, I thank her, at her Maid's Wedding, and burnt off the Handle.

BOY
I will Sir.

[Exit.

1ST CITIZEN
Who's within here, hoe Neighbor, not stirring yet?

2ND CITIZEN
Oh, good morrow, good morrow: what news, what news?

1ST CITIZEN
It holds, he dies this morning.

2ND CITIZEN
Then happy man be his fortune, I am resolv'd.

1ST CITIZEN
And so am I, and forty more good fellows, That will not give their heads for the washing, I take it.

2ND CITIZEN
'Sfoot man, who would not hang in such good company, and such a cause? A Fire, a Wife and Children; 'Tis such a jest that men should look behind 'em to the world: and let their honors, their honors neighbor, slip.

1ST CITIZEN
I'll give thee a pint of Bastard and a Roll for that bare word.

2ND CITIZEN
They say, that we Tailors, are things that lay one another, and our Geese hatch us: I'll make some of 'em feel they are Geese o'th' game then.
I'fack, take down my Bill, 'tis ten to one I use it. Take a

good heart man, all the low ward is ours, with a wet finger.
And lay my cut-fing'red Gantlet ready for me,
That, that I us'd to work in, when the Gentl. were
Up against us, and beaten out of Town, and almost out o'
Debt too: for a plague on 'em they never paid well since:
And take heed sirrah, your Mistriss hears not of this
Business, she's near her time: yet if she do,
I care not, she may long for Rebellion,
For she has a devilish spirit.

1ST CITIZEN

Come, let's call up the new Iremonger, he's as tough as steel, and has a fine wit in these resurrections;
Are you stirring neighbor?

3RD CITIZEN

Within. Oh, Good morrow neighbors, I'll come to you presently.

2ND CITIZEN

Goe to, this is his Mothers doing; she's a Polecat.

1ST CITIZEN

As any Is In the world.

2ND CITIZEN

Then say, I have hit it, and a vengeance on her, let her be what she will.

1ST CITIZEN

Amen say I, she has brought things to a fine pass with her wisdom: do you mark it?

2ND CITIZEN

One thing I am sure she has, the good old Duke, she gives him pap again they say, and dandles him, and hangs a corral and bells about his neck, and makes him believe his teeth will come agen; which if they did, and I he, I would worry her as never Curr was worried: I would neighbor, till my teeth met I know where, but that's counsel.

[Enter **3RD CITIZEN**.

3RD CITIZEN

Good morrow neighbors: hear you the sad news?

1ST CITIZEN

Yes, would we knew as well how to prevent it.

3RD CITIZEN

I cannot tell, methinks 'twere no great matter, if men were men: but—

2ND CITIZEN

You do not twit me with my calling neighbor?

3ᴿᴰ CITIZEN
No surely: for I know your spirit to be tall; pray be not vext.

2ᴺᴰ CITIZEN
Pray forward with your counsel: I am what I am, and they that prove me shall find me to their cost: do you mark me neighbor, to their cost I say.

1ˢᵀ CITIZEN
Nay, look how soon you are angry!

2ᴺᴰ CITIZEN
They shall neighbors: yes, I say they shall.

3ᴿᴰ CITIZEN
I do believe they shall.

1ˢᵀ CITIZEN
I know they shall.

2ᴺᴰ CITIZEN
Whether you do or no I care not two pence,
I am no beast, I know mine own strength neighbors;
God bless the King, your companies is fair.

1ˢᵀ CITIZEN
Nay neighbor, now ye erre, I tell you so, and ye were twenty Neighbors.

3ᴿᴰ CITIZEN
You had best goe peach, doe, peach.

2ᴺᴰ CITIZEN
Peach; I scorn the motion.

3ᴿᴰ CITIZEN
Doe, and see what follows: I'll spend an hundred pound, and be two I care not: but I'll undoe thee.

2ᴺᴰ CITIZEN
Peach, Oh disgrace! Peach in thy face, and doe the worst thou canst: I am a true-man, and a free-man: peach!

1ˢᵀ CITIZEN
Nay, look, you will spoil all.

2ᴺᴰ CITIZEN
Peach!

1ˢᵀ CITIZEN

Whilst you two brawl together, the Prince will lose his life.

3RD CITIZEN
Come, give me your hand, I love you well, are you for the action?

2ND CITIZEN
Yes: but Peach provokes me, 'tis a cold fruit, I feel it cold in my stomach still.

3RD CITIZEN
No more, I'll give you Cake to digest it.

[Enter the **4TH CITIZEN**.

4TH CITIZEN
Shut up my shop, and be ready at a call boys, and one of you run over my old tuck with a few ashes, 'tis grown odious with tosting Cheese: and burn a little Juniper in my Murrin, the Maid made it her Chamber-pot: an hour hence I'll come again; and as you hear from me, send me a clean shirt.

3RD CITIZEN
The Chandler by the Wharf, and it be thy Will.

2ND CITIZEN
Gossip, good morrow.

4TH CITIZEN
Oh good morrow Gossip: good morrow all, I see ye of one mind you cleave so close together: come 'tis time, I have prepared a hundred if they stand.

1ST CITIZEN
1. 'Tis well done: shall we sever, and about it?

3RD CITIZEN
First, let's to the Tavern, and a pint a piece will make us Dragons.

2ND CITIZEN
I will have no mercy, come what will of it.

4TH CITIZEN
If my tuck hold, I'll spit the Guard like Larks with sage between 'em.

2ND CITIZEN
I have a foolish Bill to reckon with 'em, will make some of their hearts ake, and I'll lay it on: now shall I fight, 'twill do you good to see me.

3RD CITIZEN
Come, I'll do something for the Town to talk of when I am rotten: pray God there be enough to kill, that's all.

[Exeunt.

[Enter **DORIALUS, NISUS, AGENOR**.

AGENOR
How black the day begins!

DORIALUS
Can you blame it, and look upon such a deed as shall be done this morning?

NISUS
Does the Prince suffer to day?

DORIALUS
Within this hour they say.

AGENOR
Well, they that are most wicked are most safe: 'twill be a strange justice, and a lamentable, gods keep us from the too soon feeling of it.

DORIALUS
I care not if my throat were next: for to live still, and live here, were but to grow fat for the Shambles.

NISUS
Yet we must do it, and thank 'em too, that our lives may be accepted.

AGENOR
Faith I'll go starve my self, or grow diseas'd to shame the hangman; for I am sure he shall be my Herald, and quarter me.

DORIALUS
I, a plague on him, he's too excellent at Arms.

NISUS
Will you go see this sad sight, my Lord Agenor?

AGENOR
I'll make a mourner.

DORIALUS
If I could do him any good, I would goe,
The bare sight else will but afflict my spirit,
My prayers shall be as near him as your eyes:
As you find him setled, remember my love and service to his Grace.

NISUS
We will weep for you, Sir: farewel.

[Exeunt.

DORIALUS
Farewell to all our happiness, a long farewel.
Thou angry power, whether of Heaven or Hell,
Thou laist this sharp correction on our Kingdom
For our offences, infinite and mighty!
Oh hear me, and at length be pleas'd, be pleas'd
With pity to draw back thy vengeance,
Too heavy for our weakness; and accept,
(Since it is your discretion, heavenly Wisdoms,
To have it so) this sacrifice for all,
That now is flying to your happiness,
Only for you most fit: let all our sins suffer in him.

[A shout within.

Gods, what's the matter? I hope 'tis joy;
How now my Lords?

[Enter **AGENOR** and **NISUS**.

NISUS
I'll tell you with that little breath I have;
More joy than you dare think, The Prince is safe from danger.

DORIALUS
How!

AGENOR
'Tis true, and thus it was; his hour was come
To lose his life, he ready for the stroke,
Nobly, and full of Saint-like patience,
Went with his Guard: which when the people saw,
Compassion first went out, mingled with tears,
That bred desires, and whispers to each other,
To do some worthy kindness for the Prince,
And e'r they understood well how to do,
Fury stept in, and taught them what to do,
Thrusting on every hand to rescue him,
As a white innocent: then flew the roar
Through all the streets, of Save him, save him, save him:
And as they cry'd, they did; for catching up
Such sudden weapons as their madness shew them
In short, they beat the Guard, and took him from 'em,
And now march with him like a royal Army.

DORIALUS

Heaven, heaven I thank thee,
What a slave was I to have my hand so far from
This brave rescue, 't 'ad been a thing to brag on
When I was old. Shall we run for a wager to the
Next Temple, and give thanks?

NISUS
As fast as wishes.

[Enter **LEUCIPPUS** and **ISMENUS**: the **PEOPLE** within stops.

LEUCIPPUS
Good friends goe home again, there's not a man shall goe with me.

ISMENUS
Will you not take revenge? I'll call them on.

LEUCIPPUS
All that love me, depart:
I thank you, and will serve you for your loves:
But I will thank you more to suffer me
To govern 'em: once more, I do beg ye,
For my sake to your houses.

ALL WITHIN
Gods preserve you.

ISMENUS
And what house will you goe to?

LEUCIPPUS
Ismenus, I will take the wariest courses that I can think of to defend my self, but not offend.

ISMENUS
You may kill your Mother, and never offend your Father, an honest man.

LEUCIPPUS
Thou know'st I can scape now, that's all I look for:
I'll leave.

ISMENUS
Timantus, a pox take him, would I had him here, I would kill him at his own weapon single, sithes we have built enough on him: plague on't, I'm out of all patience: discharge such an Army as this, that would have followed you without paying, Oh gods!

LEUCIPPUS
To what end should I keep 'em? I am free.

ISMENUS

Yes, free o'th' Traitors, for you are proclaim'd one.

LEUCIPPUS

Should I therefore make my self one?

ISMENUS

This is one of your moral Philosophy, is it?
Heaven bless me from subtilties to undoe my self with:
But I know, if reason her self were here,
She would not part with her own safety.

LEUCIPPUS

Well, pardon Ismenus, for I know
My courses are most just; nor will I stain 'em
With one bad action; for thy self thou know'st,
That though I may command thee, I shall be
A ready servant to thee if thou needst: and so I'll take my leave.

ISMENUS

Of whom?

LEUCIPPUS

Of thee.

ISMENUS

Heart, you shall take no leave of me.

LEUCIPPUS

Shall I not?

ISMENUS

No, by the gods shall you not: nay, if you have no more wit but to goe absolutely alone, I'll be in a little.

LEUCIPPUS

Nay, prethee good Ismenus part with me.

ISMENUS

I wonnot i'faith, never move it any more; for by this good light I wonnot.

LEUCIPPUS

This is an ill time to be thus unruly: Ismenus. You must leave me.

ISMENUS

Yes, if you can beat me away: else the gods refuse me if I will leave you till I see more reason; you sha'nt undoe your self.

LEUCIPPUS

But why wilt not leave me?

ISMENUS
Why I'll tell you: Because when you are gone, then—life, if I have not forgot my reason—hell take me: you put me out of patience so: Oh! marry when you are gone, then will your Mother (a pox confound her) she never comes in my head, but she spoils my memory too: there are a hundred reasons.

LEUCIPPUS
But shew me one.

ISMENUS
Shew you; what a stir here is; why I will shew you: Do you think; well, well, I know what I know, I pray come, come. 'Tis in vain: but I am sure. Devils take 'em; what do I meddle with 'em? You know your self. Soul, I think I am: is there any man i'th' world? as if you knew not this already better than I. Pish, pish, I'll give no reason.

LEUCIPPUS
But I will tell thee one, why thou shouldst stay:
I have not one friend in the Court but thou,
On whom I may be bold to trust to send me
Any intelligence: and if thou lov'st me
Thou wilt do this, thou needst not fear to stay,
For there are new-come Proclamations out,
Where all are pardon'd but my self.

ISMENUS
'Tis true, and in the same Proclamation, your fine Sister Urania, whom you us'd so kindly, is proclaim'd Heir apparent to the Crown.

LEUCIPPUS
What though, thou mayst stay at home without danger.

ISMENUS
Danger, hang danger, what tell you me of danger?

LEUCIPPUS
Why if thou wilt not do't, I think thou dar'st not.

ISMENUS
I dare not: if you speak it in earnest, you are a Boy.

LEUCIPPUS
Well Sir, if you dare, let me see you do't.

ISMENUS
Why so you shall, I will stay.

LEUCIPPUS

Why God-a-mercy.

ISMENUS
You know I love you but too well.

LEUCIPPUS
Now take these few directions: farewel, send to me by the wariest ways thou canst: I have a soul tells me we shall meet often. The gods protect thee.

ISMENUS
Pox o' my self for an ass, I'm crying now, God be with you, if I never see you again: why then pray get you gone, for grief and anger wonnot let me know what I say, I'll to the Court as fast as I can, and see the new Heir apparant.

[Exeunt.

ACTUS QUINTUS

SCÆNA PRIMA

Enter **URANIA** and her **WOMAN**.

URANIA
What hast thou found him?

WOMAN
Madam, he is coming in.

URANIA
Gods bless my brother, wheresoe'er he is:
And I beseech you keep me fro the bed
Of any naughty Tyrant, whom my Mother
Would ha me have to wrong him.

[Enter **ISMENUS**.

ISMENUS
What would her new Grace have with me?

URANIA
Leave us a while. My Lord Ismenus,

[Exit **WOMAN**.

I pray for the love of Heaven and God,
That you would tell me one thing, which I know

You can do weell.

ISMENUS
Where's her fain Grace?

URANIA
You know me well inough, but that you mock, I am she my sen.

ISMENUS
God bless him that shall be thy husband, if thou wear'st breeches thus soon, thou'lt be as impudent as thy Mother.

URANIA
But will you tell me this one thing?

ISMENUS
What is't? if it be no great matter whether I do or no, perhaps I will.

URANIA
Yes faith, 'tis matter.

ISMENUS
And what is't?

URANIA
I pray you let me know whaire the Prince my Brother is.

ISMENUS
I'faith you shan be hang'd first, is your Mother so foolish to think your good Grace can sift it out of me?

URANIA
If you have any mercy left i' you to a poor wench, tell me.

ISMENUS
Why wouldst not thou have thy brains beat out for this, to follow thy Mothers steps so young?

URANIA
But believe me, she knows none of this.

ISMENUS
Believe you? why do you think I never had wits? or that I am run out of them? how should it belong to you to know, if I could tell?

URANIA
Why I will tell you, and if I speak false
Let the devil ha me: yonder's a bad man,
Come from a Tyrant to my Mother, and what name
They ha' for him, good faith I cannot tell.

ISMENUS
An Ambassador.

URANIA
That's it: but he would carry me away,
And have me marry his Master; and I'll day
E'r I will ha' him.

ISMENUS
But what's this to knowing where the Prince is?

URANIA
Yes: for you know all my Mother does:
Agen the Prince is but to ma me great.

ISMENUS
Pray, I know that too well, what ten?

URANIA
Why I would goe to the good Marquis my
Brother, and put my self into his hands, that so
He may preserve himself.

ISMENUS
Oh that thou hadst no seed of thy Mother in thee, and couldst mean this now.

URANIA
Why feth I do, wou'd I might ne'er stir more if I do not.

ISMENUS
I shall prove a ridiculous fool, I'll be damn'd else: hang me if I do not half believe thee.

URANIA
By my troth you may.

ISMENUS
By my troth I doe: I know I'm an Ass for't, But I cannot help it.

URANIA
And won you tell me then?

ISMENUS
Yes faith will I, or any thing else i'th' world: for I think thou art as good a creature as ever was born.

URANIA
But ail goe i' this ladst reparrell: But you mun help me to Silver.

ISMENUS
Help thee? why the pox take him that will not help thee to any thing i'th' world, I'll help thee to Money, and I'll do't presently too, and yet soul, If you should play the scurvy Harlotry little pocky baggage now and cosin me, what then?

URANIA
Why, an I do, wou'd I might ne'r see day agen.

ISMENUS
Nay, by this light, I do not think thou wilt: I'll presently provide thee Money and a Letter.

[Exit **ISMENUS**.

URANIA
I, but I'll ne'er deliver it.
When I have found my Brother, I will beg
To serve him; but he shall never know who I am:
For he must hate me then for my bad mother:
I'll say I am a Countrey Lad that want a service,
And have straid on him by chance, lest he discover me;
I know I must not live long, but that time
I ha' to spend, shall be in serving him.
And though my Mother seek to take his life away,
In ai day my brother shall be taught
That I was ever good, though she were naught.

[Exit.

[Enter **BACHA** and **TIMANTUS**: **BACHA** reading a Letter.

BACHA
Run away, the Devil be her guide.

TIMANTUS
Faith she's gone: there's a Letter, I found it in her pocket, would I were with her, she's a handsome Lady, a plague upon my bashfulness, I had bobb'd her long ago else.

LEUCIPPUS
What a base whore is this, that after all
My ways for her advancement, should so poorly
Make virtue her undoer, and choose this time,
The King being deadly sick, and I intending
A present marriage with some forreign Prince,
To strengthen and secure my self. She writes here
Like a wise Gentlewoman, She will not stay:
And the example of her dear brother, makes her
Fear her self, to whom she means to flie.

TIMANTUS

Why, who can help it?

BACHA

Now Poverty and Lechery, which is thy end, rot thee, where e'er thou goest with all thy goodness.

TIMANTUS

Berlady they'll bruze her: and she were of brass. I am sure they'll break stone Walls: I have had experience of them both, and they have made me desperate: but there's a messenger, Madam, come from the Prince with a Letter to Ismenus, who by him returns an answer.

BACHA

This comes as pat as wishes: thou shalt presently away Timantus.

TIMANTUS

Whither Madam?

BACHA

To the Prince, and take the Messenger for guide.

TIMANTUS

What shall I do there? I have done too much mischief to be believ'd again; or indeed, to scape with my head on my back, if I be once known.

BACHA

Thou art a weak shallow fool: get thee a disguise, and withal, when thou com'st before him, have a Letter fain'd to deliver him: and then, as thou hast ever hope of goodness by me, or after me, strike one home stroke that shall not need another: dar'st thou speak, dar'st thou? if thou fall'st off, go be a Rogue again, and lie and pander to procure thy meat: dar'st thou speak to me?

TIMANTUS

Sure I shall never walk when I am dead: I have no spirit, Madam, I'll be drunk but I'll do it, that's all my refuge.

[Exit.

BACHA

Away, no more, then I'll raise an Army whilst the King yet lives, if all the means and power I have can do it, I cannot tell.

[Enter **ISMENUS** and three **LORDS**.

ISMENUS

Are you inventing still? we'll ease your studies.

BACHA

Why how now saucy Lords?

ISMENUS
Nay, I'll shake ye; yes devil, I will shake ye.

BACHA
Do not you know me Lords?

NISUS
Yes deadly sin we know ye, would we did not.

ISMENUS
Doe you hear whore, a plague a God upon thee, the Duke is dead.

LEUCIPPUS
Dead!

ISMENUS
I, wild-fire and brimstone take thee: good man he is dead, and past those miseries which thou, salt infection-like; like a disease flungst upon his head. Dost thou hear, and 'twere not more respect to Womanhood in general than thee, because I had a Mother, who I will not say she was good, she liv'd so near thy time, I would have thee in vengeance of this man, whose peace is made in heaven by this time, tied to a post; and dried i' th' sun, and after carried about, and shewn at Fairs for money, with a long story of the devil thy father, that taught thee to be whorish, envious, bloudy.

BACHA
Ha, ha, ha.

ISMENUS
You fleering harlot, I'll have a horse to leap thee, and thy base issue shall carry Sumpters. Come Lords, bring her along, we'll to the Prince all, where her hell-hood shall wait his censure; and if he spare thee she-Goat, may he lie with thee again: and beside, maist thou lay upon him some nasty foul disease, that hate still follows, and his end a dry ditch. Lead you corrupted whore, or I'll draw a goad shall make you skip: away to the Prince.

BACHA
Ha ha, ha, I hope yet I shall come too late to find him.

[Cornets. **CUPID** from above.

[Enter **LEUCIPPUS, URANIA: LEUCIPPUS** with a bloody Handkerchief.

LEUCIPPUS
Alas poor boy, why dost thou follow me?
What canst thou hope for? I am poor as thou art.

URANIA
In good feth I shall be weel and rich enough
If you will love me, and not put me from you.

LEUCIPPUS

Why dost thou choose out me Boy to undo thee?
Alas, for pitty take another Master,
That may be able to deserve thy love
In breeding thee hereafter: me thou knowest not,
More than my misery: and therefore canst not
Look for rewards at my hands: would I were able
My pretty knave, to doe thee any kindness: truly
Good Boy, I would upon my faith, thy harmless
Innocence moves me at heart: wilt thou goe
Save thy self; why dost thou weep?
Alas, I do not chide thee.

URANIA

I cannot tell if I go from you; Sir, I shall ne'er dawn day more: Pray if you can, I will be true to you: Let me wait on you: if I were a man, I would fight for you: Sure you have some ill-willers, I would slay um.

LEUCIPPUS

Such harmless souls are ever Prophets: well, I take thy wish, thou shalt be with me still: But prethee eat, then my good boy: Thou wilt die my child if thou fast one day more. This four daies thou hast tasted nothing: Goe into the Cave and eat: thou shalt find something for thee, to bring thy bloud again, and thy fair colour.

URANIA

I cannot eat, God thank you. But I'll eat to morrow.

LEUCIPPUS

Thou't be dead by that time.

URANIA

I should be well then, for you will not love me.

LEUCIPPUS

Indeed I will. This is the prettiest passion that e'er I felt yet: why dost thou look so earnestly upon me?

URANIA

You have fair eyes Master.

LEUCIPPUS

Sure the boy dotes: why dost thou sigh my child?

URANIA

To think that such a fine man should live, and no gay
Lady love him.

LEUCIPPUS

Thou wilt love me?

URANIA

Yes sure till I die, and when I am in heaven, I'll e'en wish for you.

LEUCIPPUS

And I'll come to thee boy. This is a Love I never yet heard tell of: come, thou art sleepy child; goe in, and I'll sit with thee: heaven what portends this?

URANIA

You are sad, but I am not sleepy, would I could do ought to make you merry: shall I sing?

LEUCIPPUS

If thou wilt good Boy. Alas my boy, that thou shouldst comfort me, and art far worse than I!

[Enter **TIMANTUS** with a Letter disguised.

URANIA

Law Master, there's one, look to your sen.

LEUCIPPUS

What art thou that in this dismal place,
Which nothing could find out but misery,
Thus boldly stepst? Comfort was never here,
Here is no food, nor beds, nor any house
Built by a better Architect than beasts;
And e'r you get dwelling from one of them,
You must fight for it: if you conquer him,
He is your meat: if not, you must be his.

TIMANTUS

I come to you (for if I not mistake, you are the
Prince) from that most Noble Lord Ismenus with a Letter.

URANIA

Alas, I fear I shall be discover'd now.

LEUCIPPUS

Now I feel my self the poorest of all mortal things.
Where is he that receives such courtesies
But he has means to shew his gratefulness
Some way or other? I have none at all:
I know not how to speak so much as well
Of thee, but to these trees.

[**LEUCIPPUS** opening the Letter, the whilst **TIMANTUS** runs at him, and **URANIA** steps before.

TIMANTUS

His Letters speak him, Sir—

URANIA

Gods keep me but from knowing him till I die: aye me, sure I cannot live a day, Oh thou foul Traitor: How do you Master?

LEUCIPPUS

How dost thou my child? alas, look on this, it may make thee repentant, to behold those innocent drops that thou hast drawn from thence.

URANIA

'Tis nothing Sir, and you be well.

TIMANTUS

Oh pardon me, know you me now, Sir?

LEUCIPPUS

How couldst thou find me out?

TIMANTUS

We intercepted a Letter from Ismenus, and the bearer directed me.

LEUCIPPUS

Stand up Timantus boldly,
The world conceives that thou art guilty
Of divers treasons to the State and me:
But oh far be it from the innocence
Of a just man, to give a Traitor death
Without a tryal: here the Countrey is not
To purge thee or condemn thee; therefore
A nobler trial than thou dost deserve,
Rather than none at all, here I accuse thee
Before the face of Heaven, to be a Traitor
Both to the Duke my Father and to me, and the
Whole Land: speak, is it so or no?

TIMANTUS

'Tis true Sir, pardon me.

LEUCIPPUS

Take heed Timantus how thou dost cast away thy self, I must proceed to execution hastily if thou confess it: speak once againe, is it so or no?

TIMANTUS

I am not guilty, Sir.

[Fight here: the **PRINCE** gets his sword, and gives it him.

LEUCIPPUS

Gods and thy sword acquit thee, here it is.

TIMANTUS
I will not use any violence against your Highness.

LEUCIPPUS
At thy peril then, for this must be thy trial: and from henceforth look to thy self.

[**TIMANTUS** draws his sword, and runs at him when he turns aside.

TIMANTUS
I do beseech you, Sir, let me not fight.

LEUCIPPUS
Up, up again Timantus,
There is no way but this, believe me.
Now if—Fie, fie Timantus, is there no
Usage can recover thee from baseness? wert thou
Longer to converse with men, I would have chid
Thee for this: be all thy faults forgiven.

TIMANTUS
Oh spare me Sir, I am not fit for death,

LEUCIPPUS
I think thou art not, yet trust me, fitter than for life: Yet tell me e'r thy breath be gone, know'st of any other plots against me?

TIMANTUS
Of none.

LEUCIPPUS
What course wouldst thou have taken, when thou hadst kill'd me?

TIMANTUS
I would have ta'en your Page, and married her.

LEUCIPPUS
What Page?

TIMANTUS
Your boy there.

[Dies.

[**URANIA** sounds.

LEUCIPPUS
Is he fall'n mad in death, what does he mean?

Some good god help me at the worst: how dost thou?
Let not thy misery vex me, thou shalt have
What thy poor heart can wish: I am a Prince,
And I will keep thee in the gayest cloaths,
And the finest things, that ever pretty boy had given him.

URANIA
I know you well enough,
Feth I am dying, and now you know all too.

LEUCIPPUS
But stir up thy self; look what a Jewel here is,
See how it glisters: what a pretty shew
Will this make in thy little ear? ha, speak,
Eat but a bit, and take it.

URANIA
Do you not know me?

LEUCIPPUS
I prethee mind thy health: why that's well said my good boy, smile still.

URANIA
I shall smile till death an I see you, I am Urania,
your Sister-in-law.

LEUCIPPUS
How?

URANIA
I am Urania.

LEUCIPPUS
Dulness did seize me, now I know thee well;
Alas, why cam'st thou hither?

URANIA
Feth for love, I would not let you know till I was dying; for you could not love me, my Mother was so
naught.

LEUCIPPUS
I will love thee, or any thing: what? wilt
Thou leave me as soon as I know thee?
Speak one word to me: alas she's past it,
She will ne'er speak more.
What noise is that? it is no matter who

[Enter **ISMENUS** with the **LORDS**.

Comes on me now. What worse than mad are you
That seek out sorrows? if you love delights
Begone from hence.

ISMENUS
Sir, for you we come, as Soldiers to revenge the wrongs you have suffer'd under this naughty creature:
what shall be done with her? say, I am ready.

LEUCIPPUS
Leave her to Heaven, brave Cosin, they shall tell her how she has sinn'd against 'em, my hand shall never
be stain'd with such base bloud: live wicked Mother: that reverend Title be your pardon, for I will use no
extremity against you, but leave you to Heaven.

BACHA
Hell take you all, or if there be a place
Of torment that exceeds that, get you thither:
And till the devils have you, may your lives
Be one continued plague, and such a one,
That knows no friends nor ending.
May all ages that shall succeed, curse you as I do:
And if it be possible, I ask it heaven,
That your base issues may be ever Monsters,
That must for shame of nature and succession,
Be drown'd like dogs.
Would I had breath to poyson you.

LEUCIPPUS
Would you had love within you, and such grief
As might become a Mother: look you there,
Know you that face? that was Urania:
These are the fruits of those unhappy Mothers,
That labour with such horrid births as you do:
If you can weep, there's cause; poor innocent,
Your wickedness has kill'd her: I'll weep for you.

ISMENUS
Monstrous woman,
Mars would weep at this, and yet she cannot.

LEUCIPPUS
Here lies your Minion too, slain by my hand,
I will not say you are the cause: yet certain,
I know you were to blame, the gods forgive you.

ISMENUS
See, she stands as if she were inventing
Some new destruction for the world.

LEUCIPPUS

Ismenus, thou art welcome yet to my sad company.

ISMENUS

I come to make you somewhat sadder, Sir.

LEUCIPPUS

You cannot, I am at the height already.

ISMENUS

Your Fathers dead.

LEUCIPPUS

I thought so, Heaven be with him: Oh woman, woman, weep now or never, thou hast made more sorrows than we have eyes to utter.

BACHA

Now let Heaven fall, I am at the worst of evils, a thing so miserably wretched, that every thing, the last of humane comforts hath left me: I will not be so base and cold, to live and wait the mercies of these men I hate, no, 'tis just I die, since fortune hath left me, my step discent attends me: hand, strike thou home, I have soul enough to guide; and let all know, as I stood a Queen, the same I'll fall, and one with me.

[She stabs the **PRINCE** with a knife.

LEUCIPPUS

Ho.

ISMENUS

How do you, Sir?

LEUCIPPUS

Nearer my health, than I think any here, my tongue begins to faulter: what is man? or who would be one, when he sees a poor weak woman can in an instant make him none.

DORIALUS

She is dead already.

ISMENUS

Let her be damn'd already as she is: post all for Surgeons.

LEUCIPPUS

Let not a man stirr, for I am but dead:
I have some few words which I would have you hear,
And am afraid I shall want breath to speak 'em:
First to you my Lords, you know Ismenus is

Undoubtedly Heir of Lycia, I do beseech you all,
When I am dead, to shew your duties to him.

LORDS
We vow to do't.

LEUCIPPUS
I thank you.
Next to you Cosin Ismenus, that shall be the Duke,
I pray you let the broken Image of Cupid
Be re-edified, I know all this is done by him.

ISMENUS
It shall be so.

LEUCIPPUS
Last, I beseech you that my Mother-in-law may have a burial according to—

[Dies.

ISMENUS
To what, Sir?

DORIALUS
There is a full point.

ISMENUS
I will interpret for him; she shall have burial according to her own deserts, with dogs.

DORIALUS
I would your Majesty would haste for setling of the people.

ISMENUS
I am ready.

AGENOR
Goe, and let the Trumpets sound
Some mournful thing, whilst we convey the body
Of this unhappy Prince unto the Court,
And of that virtuous Virgin to a Grave:
But drag her to a ditch, where let her lie,
Accurst, whilst one man has a memory.

[Exeunt.

CUPID'S Speech.

The time now of my Revenge draws near.
Nor shall it lessen as I am a god,
With all the cries and prayers that have been;
And those that be to come, though they be infinite,
In need and number.

Francis Beaumont – A Short Biography

Francis Beaumont was born in 1584 near the small Leicestershire village of Thringstone. Unfortunately precise records of much of his short life do not exist.

He was the son to Sir Francis Beaumont of Grace Dieu, a justice of the common pleas. His mother was Anne, the daughter of Sir George Pierrepont.

The first date we can give for his education is at age 13 when he begins at Broadgates Hall (now Pembroke College, Oxford). Sadly, his father died the following year, 1598. Beaumont left university without a degree and entered the Inner Temple in London in 1600. A career choice of Law taken previously by his father.

The information to hand is confident that Beaumont's career in law was short-lived. He was quickly attracted to the theatre and soon became first an admirer and then a student of poet and playwright Ben Jonson. Jonson at this time was a cultural behemoth; very talented and a life full of volatility that included frequent brushes with the authorities. His followers, including the poet Robert Herrick, were known as 'the sons of Ben'. Beaumont was also on friendly terms with other luminaries such as the poet Michael Drayton.

Beaumont's first work was Salmacis and Hermaphroditus, it debuted in 1602. A 1911 edition of the Encyclopædia Britannica includes the description "not on the whole discreditable to a lad of eighteen, fresh from the popular love-poems of Marlowe and Shakespeare, which it naturally exceeds in long-winded and fantastic diffusion of episodes and conceits."

By 1605, Beaumont had written commendatory verses to Volpone one of Ben Jonson's masterpieces.

It was now, in the early years of the 17th Century, that he met John Fletcher and together they gradually formed one of the most dynamic and productive of writing teams that English theatre has ever produced.

Their playwriting careers at this stage were both troubled by early failure. Beaumont had written The Knight of the Burning Pestle and it was first performed by the Children of the Blackfriars company in 1607. The audience however was distinctly unimpressed. The publisher's epistle in the 1613 quarto says they failed to note "the privie mark of irony about it."

The following year, Fletcher's Faithful Shepherdess failed on the same stage.

In 1609, however, the two collaborated in earnest on Philaster. The play was performed by the King's Men at the Globe Theatre and at Blackfriars. It was a great success. Their careers were now well and truly launched and into the bargain they had ignited and captured a public taste for tragicomedy.

There is an account that at the time the two men shared everything. They lived together in a house on the Bankside in Southwark, " they also lived together in Bankside, sharing clothes and having "one wench in the house between them." Or as another account puts it "sharing everything in the closest intimacy."

This arrangement stopped in about 1613 when Beaumont married Ursula Isley, daughter and co-heiress of Henry Isley of Sundridge in Kent, by whom he had two daughters (one of them was born after his death).

Beaumont, at a very young age even for those times, was struck down by a stroke at some point in mid-1613, after which he was unable to write any more plays, but he did manage to write an elegy for Lady Penelope Clifton, who had died on 26th October 1613.

Francis Beaumont died on March 6th, 1616 and was buried in Westminster Abbey.

In his short life his canon was small but influential. Although he is seen more as a dramatist his poetry was celebrated even then and it continues to gain an avid readership to this day.

It was said at one point of the collaboration of Beaumont and Fletcher that "in their joint plays their talents are so ... completely merged into one, that the hand of Beaumont cannot clearly be distinguished from that of Fletcher." Whilst it was the view then it has not endured into modern times. Indeed, slowly but with certainty the name of Beaumont has been removed from many of their joint works. It has given way to other such luminaries as Philip Massinger, Nathan field and James Shirley.

John Fletcher – A Short Biography

John Fletcher was born in December, 1579 in Rye, Sussex. He was baptised on December 20th.

As can be imagined details of much of his life and career have not survived and, accordingly, only a very brief indication of his life and works can be given.

His father, Richard Fletcher, was a successful and rather ambitious cleric. From being the Dean of Peterborough he moved on to become the Bishop of Bristol, Bishop of Worcester and finally, shortly before his death, the Bishop of London. He was also the chaplain to Queen Elizabeth.

When he was Dean of Peterborough, Richard Fletcher, witnessed the execution of Mary, Queen of Scots. It was said he "knelt down on the scaffold steps and started to pray out loud and at length, in a prolonged and rhetorical style, as though determined to force his way into the pages of history". He cried out at her death, "So perish all the Queen's enemies!" All very dramatic but the family did have strong links to the Arts.

Young Fletcher appears at the very young age of eleven to have entered Corpus Christi College at Cambridge University in 1591. There are no records that he ever took a degree but there is some small evidence that he was being prepared for a career in the church.

However, what is clear is that this was soon abandoned as he joined the stream of people who would leave University and decamp to the more bohemian life of commercial theatre in London.

Unfortunately, his father fell out with Queen Elizabeth but appears to have been on his way to rehabilitation before his death in 1596. At his death he was, however, mired in debt.

The upbringing of the now teenage Fletcher and his seven siblings now passed to his paternal uncle, the poet and minor official Giles Fletcher. Giles, who had the patronage of the Earl of Essex may have been a liability rather than an advantage to the young Fletcher. With Essex involved in the failed rebellion against Elizabeth Giles was also tainted by association.

By 1606 John Fletcher appears to have equipped himself with the talents to become a playwright. Initially this appears to have been for the Children of the Queen's Revels, then performing at the Blackfriars Theatre.

Commendatory verses by Richard Brome in the Beaumont and Fletcher 1647 folio place Fletcher in the company of Ben Jonson, although it is not known when this friendship began. Jonson, of course, was a leviathan of English Literature, so admired that many of his literary friends and colleagues were simply known as 'Sons of Ben'. Fletcher's frequent early collaborator, Francis Beaumont, was also a friend of Jonson's.

Fletcher's early career was marked by one significant failure; The Faithful Shepherdess, his adaptation of Giovanni Battista Guarini's Il Pastor Fido, which was performed by the Blackfriars Children in 1608. In the preface to the printed edition of his play, Fletcher explained the failure as due to his audience's faulty expectations. They expected a pastoral tragicomedy to feature dances, comedy, and murder, with the shepherds presented in conventional stereotypes – as Fletcher put it, wearing "gray cloaks, with curtailed dogs in strings." Fletcher's preface is however best known for its pithy definition of tragicomedy: "A tragicomedy is not so called in respect of mirth and killing, but in respect it wants [i.e., lacks] deaths, which is enough to make it no tragedy; yet brings some near it, which is enough to make it no comedy." A comedy, he went on to say, must be "a representation of familiar people." His preface is critical of drama that features characters whose action violates nature.

In that case, Fletcher appears to have been developing a new style faster than audiences could comprehend. By 1609, however, he had found his stride. With Beaumont, he wrote Philaster, which became a hit for the King's Men and began a profitable association between Fletcher and that company. Philaster appears also to have begun a trend for tragicomedy. Fletcher's influence has also been said to have inspired some features of Shakespeare's late romances, and certainly his influence on the tragicomic work of other playwrights is even more marked.

By the middle of the 1610s, Fletcher's plays had achieved a popularity that rivalled Shakespeare's and cemented the pre-eminence of the King's Men in Jacobean London. After Beaumont's retirement, necessitated by ill-health, and then his early death in 1616, Fletcher continued working, both singly and in collaboration, until his death in 1625. By that time, he had produced, or had been credited with, close to fifty plays. This body of work remained a major part of the King's Men's repertory until the closing of the theatres in 1642 due to the Civil War.

At the beginning of his career Fletcher's most important collaborator was Francis Beaumont. The two wrote together for close to a decade, first for the Children of the Queen's Revels, and then for the King's Men. According to an anecdote transmitted or invented by John Aubrey, they also lived together in Bankside, sharing clothes and having "one wench in the house between them." This domestic arrangement, if it existed, was ended by Beaumont's marriage in 1613, and their dramatic partnership ended after Beaumont fell ill, probably of a stroke, that same year.

At this point Fletcher had written many plays with Beaumont and several others on his own. He seems to have been regarded as quite a talent although it should be remembered that playwrights were required to be prolific, to easily work with other collaborators and to produce work of quality and commercial appeal very quickly.

The King's Men, run by Philip Henslowe, was the most prestigious of the theatre companies and Fletcher now had an increasingly close association with it.

Fletcher collaborated with Shakespeare on Henry VIII, The Two Noble Kinsmen, and the now lost Cardenio, which some scholars say was the basis for Lewis Theobald's play Double Falsehood. (Theobald is regarded as one of the best Shakespearean editors. Whether his play is based on Cardenio or on some other is not absolutely known although Theobald certainly promoted it as his revision of the lost Shakespeare/Fletcher play.)

A play that Fletcher also wrote by himself at this time, The Woman's Prize or the Tamer Tamed, is also regarded as a sequel to The Taming of the Shrew.

In 1616, with the death of Shakespeare, Fletcher now appears to have entered into an enhanced arrangement with the King's Men on very similar terms to Shakespeare's. Fletcher would now write exclusively for the King's Men until his own death almost a decade later.

As well as continuing his solo productions Fletcher was still collaborating with other playwrights, mainly Philip Massinger, who, in turn, would succeed him as the in-house playwright for the King's Men.

Fletcher's popularity continued throughout his life; indeed, during the winter of 1621, he had three of his plays performed at court. His mastery is most notable in two dramatic types; tragicomedy and the comedy of manners.

John Fletcher died in 1625, it is thought of bubonic plague which, at the time, was undergoing further outbreaks.

He seems to have been buried in what is now Southwark Cathedral, although a precise location is not known. There is much made of an anecdote that Fletcher and Massinger (who died in 1640) share the same grave but it is more likely that both are buried within a few yards of each other and that the stone markers in the floor have confused the issue. One is marked 'Edmond Shakespeare 1607' and the other 'John Fletcher 1625' refers to Shakespeare's younger brother and the playwright. The churchyards were, more often than not, completely over-crowded and breeding grounds for disease. Precise record keeping was not a practiced skill.

During the later Commonwealth, many of the playwright's best-known scenes were kept alive as drolls. These were brief performances, usually condensed into one or two scenes and with the addition of music or song to satisfy the taste for plays while the theatres were closed under the Puritans. At the re-opening of the theatres in 1660, the plays in the Fletcher canon, in original form or revised, were by far the most common productions on the English stage. The most frequently revived plays suggest the developing taste for comedies of manners. Among the tragedies, The Maid's Tragedy and, especially, Rollo Duke of Normandy held the stage. Four tragicomedies (A King and No King, The Humorous Lieutenant, Philaster, and The Island Princess) were popular, perhaps in part for their similarity to and foreshadowing of heroic drama. Four comedies (Rule a Wife And Have a Wife, The Chances, Beggars' Bush, and especially The Scornful Lady) were also stage mainstays.

Despite his popularity, and it appears he was held in higher regard than Shakespeare at this time, his works steadily lost ground to those of Shakespeare and to new productions from other playwrights.

Since then Fletcher has increasingly become a subject only for occasional revivals and for specialists. Fletcher and his collaborators have been the subject of important bibliographic and critical studies, but the plays have been revived only infrequently.

Due to the frequent collaborations between all manner of playwrights, and the revisions carried out in later years, having a settled list of authorship to any given set of plays can be problematic. The works of Fletcher and others of this period most definitely fall into this category. It is as well to take into account that during this period theatres were quite often closed either due to outbreaks of the plague or to the prevailing political and moral climate. Printers, anxious to provide materials that would sell, were not above changing a name or two to enhance sales.

Although Fletcher collaborated most often with Beaumont and Massinger, it is believed that Massinger revised many of the plays some time after their original production. Other collaborators including Nathan Field, William Shakespeare, William Rowley and others also can be seen distinctly in Fletchers' works. Many modern scholars point out that Fletcher had many particular mannerisms, but other playwrights would also duplicate these at times so allocating exact contributions of anyone to a play is somewhat of a detective case in many instances. However, from the original folio printings or licensing via the Master of the Revels (the statutory licensing authority to approve and censor plays as well a hand in publication and printing of theatrical materials) as well as contemporary notes a fairly precise bibliography of the works can be given with only a few plays lacking substantial authority and provenance.

Francis Beaumont & John Fletcher – A Concise Bibliography

This bibliography gives the most likely date of writing together with when published, revised or licensed by the Master or the Revels (This position within the royal household was originally for royal festivities, ie revels, and later to oversee stage censorship, until this function was transferred to the Lord Chamberlain in 1624).

Francis Beaumont – Solo Plays
The Knight of the Burning Pestle, comedy (performed 1607; printed 1613)

The Masque of the Inner Temple and Gray's Inn, masque (printed 1613)

John Fletcher - Solo Plays
The Faithful Shepherdess, pastoral (written 1608–9; printed 1609)
The Tragedy of Valentinian, tragedy (1610–14; 1647)
Monsieur Thomas, comedy (c. 1610–16; 1639)
The Woman's Prize, or The Tamer Tamed, comedy (c. 1611; 1647)
Bonduca, tragedy (1611–14; 1647)
The Chances, comedy (c. 1613–25; 1647)
Wit Without Money, comedy (c. 1614; 1639)
The Mad Lover, tragicomedy (acted 5 January 1617; 1647)
The Loyal Subject, tragicomedy (licensed 16 November 1618; revised 1633; 1647)
The Humorous Lieutenant, tragicomedy (c. 1619; 1647)
Women Pleased, tragicomedy (c. 1619–23; 1647)
The Island Princess, tragicomedy (c. 1620; 1647)
The Wild Goose Chase, comedy (c. 1621; 1652)
The Pilgrim, comedy (c. 1621; 1647)
A Wife for a Month, tragicomedy (licensed 27 May 1624; 1647)
Rule a Wife and Have a Wife, comedy (licensed 19 October 1624; 1640)

Francis Beaumont & John Fletcher
The Woman Hater, comedy (1606; 1607)
Cupid's Revenge, tragedy (c. 1607–12; 1615)
Philaster, or Love Lies a-Bleeding, tragicomedy (c. 1609; 1620)
The Maid's Tragedy, Tragedy (c. 1609; 1619)
A King and No King, tragicomedy (1611; 1619)
The Captain, comedy (c. 1609–12; 1647)
The Scornful Lady, comedy (c. 1613; 1616)
Love's Pilgrimage, tragicomedy (c. 1615–16; 1647)
The Noble Gentleman, comedy (c. 1613; licensed 3 February 1626; 1647)

Their Collaborations with Others

With Philip Massinger
Thierry & Theodoret, tragedy (c. 1607; 1621)
The Coxcomb, comedy (c. 1608–10; 1647)
Beggars' Bush, comedy (c. 1612–13; revised 1622; 1647)
Love's Cure, comedy (c. 1612–13; revised 1625; 1647)

John Fletcher with Philip Massinger
Sir John van Olden Barnavelt, tragedy (August 1619; MS)
The Little French Lawyer, comedy (c. 1619–23; 1647)
A Very Woman, tragicomedy (c. 1619–22; licensed 6 June 1634; 1655)
The Custom of the Country, comedy (c. 1619–23; 1647)
The Double Marriage, tragedy (c. 1619–23; 1647)
The False One, history (c. 1619–23; 1647)
The Prophetess, tragicomedy (licensed 14 May 1622; 1647)
The Sea Voyage, comedy (licensed 22 June 1622; 1647)

The Spanish Curate, comedy (licensed 24 October 1622; 1647)
The Lovers' Progress or The Wandering Lovers, tragicomedy (licensed 6 December 1623; rev 1634; 1647)
The Elder Brother, comedy (c. 1625; 1637)

John Fletcher with Philip Massinger & Nathan Field
The Honest Man's Fortune, tragicomedy (1613; 1647)
The Queen of Corinth, tragicomedy (c. 1616–18; 1647)
The Knight of Malta, tragicomedy (c. 1619; 1647)

John Fletcher with William Shakespeare
Henry VIII, history (c. 1613; 1623)
The Two Noble Kinsmen, tragicomedy (c. 1613; 1634)
Cardenio, tragicomedy (c. 1613)

John Fletcher with Thomas Middleton & William Rowley
Wit at Several Weapons, comedy (c. 1610–20; 1647)

John Fletcher with William Rowley
The Maid in the Mill (licensed 29 August 1623; 1647).

John Fletcher with Nathan Field
Four Plays, or Moral Representations, in One, morality (c. 1608–13; 1647)

John Fletcher with Philip Massinger, Ben Jonson and George Chapman
Rollo Duke of Normandy, or The Bloody Brother, tragedy (c. 1617; revised 1627–30; 1639)

John Fletcher with James Shirley
The Night Walker, or The Little Thief, comedy (c. 1611; 1640)
The Coronation c. 1635

Uncertain
The Nice Valour, or The Passionate Madman, comedy (c. 1615–25; 1647)
The Laws of Candy, tragicomedy (c. 1619–23; 1647)
The Fair Maid of the Inn, comedy (licensed 22 January 1626; 1647)
The Faithful Friends, tragicomedy (registered 29 June 1660; MS.)

The Nice Valour is possibly by Fletcher revised by Thomas Middleton;

The Fair Maid of the Inn is perhaps a play by Massinger, John Ford, and John Webster, either with or without Fletcher's involvement.

The Laws of Candy has been variously attributed to Fletcher and to John Ford.

The Night-Walker was a Fletcher original, with additions by Shirley for a 1639 production.

Even now there is not absolute certainty on several of the plays. The first Beaumont & Fletcher folio of 1647 contained 35 plays and the second folio of 1679 added a further 18. In total 53 plays.

The first folio included The Masque of the Inner Temple and Gray's Inn (1613), and the second The Knight of the Burning Pestle (1607), widely considered Beaumont's solo works, although the latter was in early editions attributed to both writers. Fletcher himself said that Beaumont was attributed co-authorship of many works that belonged solely to Fletcher or to other collaborators.

One play in the canon, Sir John Van Olden Barnavelt, existed in manuscript and was not published till 1883.

www.ingramcontent.com/pod-product-compliance
Lightning Source LLC
Chambersburg PA
CBHW060127050426
42448CB00010B/2031